SOMALIA:
CHALLENGES AND
DEVELOPMENT EFFORTS

SOMALIA: CHALLENGES AND DEVELOPMENT EFFORTS

U.S. GOVERNMENT ACCOUNTABILITY OFFICE

Novinka Books
New York

For permission to use material from this book please contact us:
Telephone 631-231-7269; Fax 631-231-8175
Web Site: http://www.novapublishers.com

NOTICE TO THE READER

The Publisher has taken reasonable care in the preparation of this book, but makes no expressed or implied warranty of any kind and assumes no responsibility for any errors or omissions. No liability is assumed for incidental or consequential damages in connection with or arising out of information contained in this book. The Publisher shall not be liable for any special, consequential, or exemplary damages resulting, in whole or in part, from the readers' use of, or reliance upon, this material.

This publication is designed to provide accurate and authoritative information with regard to the subject matter covered herein. It is sold with the clear understanding that the Publisher is not engaged in rendering legal or any other professional services. If legal or any other expert assistance is required, the services of a competent person should be sought. FROM A DECLARATION OF PARTICIPANTS JOINTLY ADOPTED BY A COMMITTEE OF THE AMERICAN BAR ASSOCIATION AND A COMMITTEE OF PUBLISHERS.

LIBRARY OF CONGRESS CATALOGING-IN-PUBLICATION DATA
Somalia : challenges and development efforts / G.A.O. (editor).
     p. cm.
  "This book is an excerpted, indexed edition of GAO Report GAO-08-351, dated February 2008."
  ISBN 978-1-60456-778-6 (softcover)
 1. Somalia--Politics and government--1991- 2. United States--Foreign relations--Somalia. 3. Somalia--Foreign relations--United States. I. United States. Government Accountability Office.
DT407.4.S65   2008
327.7306773--dc22   2008023182

Published by Nova Science Publishers, Inc. ✤ *New York*

CONTENTS

Preface	vii
Letter	1
Results in Brief	5
Background	9
Several Challenges Have Limited U.S. and International Efforts to Stabilize Somalia	15
Insecurity and Other Challenges Have Limited the International Community's Efforts to Provide Humanitarian and Development Assistance to Somalia	23
U.S. Strategic Planning for Somalia Is Incomplete	35
Conclusions	41
Recommendation for Executive Action	43
Appendix I. Objectives, Scope, and Methodology	45
Appendix II. GAO's Description of the Six Characteristics of an Effective National Strategy	51

Appendix III.   **57**
Extent to Which the Comprehensive Regional Strategy on
Somalia Addresses GAO's Desirable Characteristics

References   **59**

Index   **65**

PREFACE

Somalia has lacked a functioning central government since 1991. In December 2006, the Ethiopian military intervened in Somalia to support Somalia's transitional government, opening what many considered a window of opportunity to rebuild the country and restore effective governance. The United States has been the largest bilateral donor to Somalia, providing roughly $362 million in assistance since 2001. In this book, the author assesses (1) U.S. and international efforts to stabilize Somalia, (2) U.S. and international efforts to provide humanitarian and development assistance to Somalia, and (3) strategic planning efforts to guide U.S. activities related to Somalia.

WHY GAO DID THIS STUDY

Somalia has lacked a functioning central government since 1991. In December 2006, the Ethiopian military intervened in Somalia to support Somalia's transitional government, opening what many considered a window of opportunity to rebuild the country and restore effective governance. The United States has been the largest bilateral donor to Somalia, providing roughly $362 million in assistance since 2001. In this report, the U.S. Government Accountability Office (GAO) assesses (1) U.S. and international efforts to stabilize Somalia, (2) U.S. and international efforts to provide humanitarian and development assistance to Somalia, and (3) strategic planning efforts to guide U.S. activities related to Somalia. GAO reviewed documents from U.S. and international organizations; interviewed U.S., United Nations (UN), Somali, and other officials; and conducted fieldwork in Kenya and Ethiopia. GAO assessed U.S. strategy using the six desirable characteristics of an effective national strategy that GAO previously developed.

WHAT GAO FOUND

Several challenges have limited U.S. and international efforts to stabilize Somalia. The international community, including the United States, is seeking to improve the security situation in the country, mainly by funding an African Union peacekeeping operation. However, a shortage of troops has hindered peacekeepers' ability to achieve their mission. In addition, the most recent attempt at political reconciliation was limited, in part because several important opposition groups were not involved. For example, while this key attempt resulted in resolutions to end the conflict and return all property to its rightful owners, these opposition groups denounced the resolutions, citing their lack of participation in drafting them. According to many officials, Somalia's Transitional Federal Government lacks institutional structures and national acceptance, and these weaknesses, in our view, have constrained U.S. and international efforts to establish the transitional government as a fully functioning central government. To mitigate these challenges, the international community, including the United States, is taking steps that include encouraging all parties to participate in reconciliation discussions.

While the international community, including the United States, continues to provide vital humanitarian and development assistance to Somalia, its efforts have been limited by lack of security, access to vulnerable populations, and effective government institutions. The international community's humanitarian assistance to Somalia, which primarily consists of food aid, has not reduced the country's acute malnutrition rates, which have remained above the emergency threshold in some parts of the country. According to UN officials, however, malnutrition is the result of a combination of immediate and underlying causes, including insufficient dietary intake, inadequate health care, and inadequate water and sanitation services. Ongoing insecurity constrains the international community's ability to monitor its provision of humanitarian and development assistance to Somalia. Furthermore, U.S. officials' inability to travel to the country has prevented them from independently monitoring assistance. The international community's plans to increase development assistance to Somalia depend on political progress and stability, which have not yet been achieved.

U.S. strategy for Somalia, outlined in the Administration's 2007 report to Congress on its Comprehensive Regional Strategy on Somalia (the Comprehensive Strategy), is incomplete. While the Comprehensive Strategy addresses the components required of it by U.S. law, it does not include the full range of U.S. government activities related to Somalia, such as DOD efforts to promote regional stability, and it does not reference other key U.S. government strategic documents for Somalia. Furthermore, the Comprehensive Strategy does not fully address any of the six desirable characteristics of an effective national strategy, lacking information on necessary resources, investments, and risk management. A separate, classified report provides more information on selected U.S. strategic planning efforts for Somalia.

ABBREVIATIONS

AMISOM	African Union Mission in Somalia
CAP	Consolidated Appeals Process
CJTF-HOA	Combined Joint Task Force-Horn of Africa
DOD	Department of Defense
FTS	Financial Tracking Service
IDP	internally displaced person
NGO	nongovernmental organization
NRC	National Reconciliation Congress
NSC	National Security Council
OCHA	United Nations Office for the Coordination of Humanitarian Affairs
RDP	Reconstruction and Development Program
SACB	Somalia Aid Coordination Body
TFG	Transitional Federal Government
UN	United Nations
UNDPKO	United Nations Department of Peacekeeping Operations
UNDP	United Nations Development Program
UNPOS	United Nations Political Office for Somalia
UNHCR	United Nations High Commissioner for Refugees
USAID	United States Agency for International Development
WFP	World Food Program

LETTER*

February 19, 2008

The Honorable Russell D. Feingold
Chairman
Subcommittee on African Affairs
Committee on Foreign Relations
United States Senate

The Honorable Donald M. Payne
Chairman
Subcommittee on Africa and Global Health
Committee on Foreign Affairs
House of Representatives

Somalia has lacked a functioning central government since 1991, when armed opposition groups' overthrow of the existing government resulted in turmoil, factional fighting, and anarchy. Somalia's current transitional government is the result of a national reconciliation process, 1 of 15 such efforts since 1991. Many observers believed a window of opportunity to rebuild Somalia and restore effective governance had opened up in December 2006, when the Ethiopian National Defense Force intervened in Somalia in support of the weak transitional government. Although an African Union peacekeeping mission was deployed to Somalia in March 2007, an ongoing insurgency against the transitional government and Ethiopian forces has contributed to continued instability in the country. In addition, floods and droughts have compounded the prolonged humanitarian emergency, with as many as 2 million people in need of humanitarian assistance. Some United Nations (UN) officials have stated that the situation in Somalia is the worst in Africa. Moreover, the U.S. government reported that the instability in Somalia has provided sanctuary to al Qaeda operatives allegedly involved in the bombings of U.S. embassies in Kenya and Tanzania in 1998.

In February 2007, in response to U.S. legislation,[1] the Administration issued the Comprehensive Regional Strategy on Somalia (Comprehensive Strategy), which lists three objectives: (1) to eliminate the terrorist threat, (2) to promote political stability, and (3) to address the humanitarian needs of the Somali people. The United States has been the largest government donor to Somalia since 2001, providing approximately $362 million in humanitarian and development assistance, mostly in food aid, through the U.S. Agency for International Development (USAID) and the Department of State (State). The United States has also provided roughly $60 million to support the African Union peacekeeping mission in Somalia. The Department of Defense (DOD) conducts a variety of regional civil affairs and humanitarian assistance operations in countries neighboring Somalia out of Djibouti.

In this report, we assess (1) the efforts of the international community, including the United States, to stabilize Somalia by improving security and political conditions; (2) the efforts of the international community, including the United States, to provide humanitarian and development assistance to Somalia; and (3) strategic planning efforts to guide U.S. activities related to Somalia. We are also issuing a separate, classified report on selected U.S. strategic planning efforts for Somalia.

To assess U.S. and international stabilization, humanitarian, and development efforts in Somalia, we obtained data, reports, and contracts from and interviewed officials at State; USAID; DOD; the National Security Council (NSC); the Transitional Federal Government (TFG) of Somalia; the governments of Ethiopia and key donor countries; and numerous international organizations, including UN agencies, the World Bank, the African Union, and nongovernmental organizations (NGO) in Washington, D.C.; New York; Nairobi, Kenya; and Addis Ababa, Ethiopia. We did not travel to Somalia due to restrictions on official U.S. government travel to the country. We also analyzed State, USAID, and DOD financial obligations for

---

* This book is an excerpted, indexed edition of GAO Report GAO-08-351, Dated February 2008

Somalia-related programs and UN-reported financial obligations from the international community to Somalia from 2001 to 2007. To assess the United States' strategic planning efforts, we examined the Comprehensive Strategy and supporting documents. We compared the strategy against the components required of it by U.S. law and assessed it using the six desirable characteristics of an effective national strategy, which we previously developed and used in several other contexts. The characteristics are (1) clear purpose, scope, and methodology; (2) detailed discussion of problems, risks, and threats; (3) desired goals, objectives, activities, and performance measures; (4) description of resources, investments, and risk management; (5) delineation of U.S. government roles, responsibilities, and coordination mechanism; and (6) description of the strategy's integration among and with other entities. We also spoke with officials from State, USAID, DOD, and NSC, and experts about the strategic planning process that resulted in the U.S. strategy for Somalia. We did not include covert activities conducted by U.S. government agencies in our review. We conducted this performance audit from January 2007 to February 2008 in accordance with generally accepted government auditing standards. Those standards require that we plan and perform the audit to obtain sufficient, appropriate evidence to provide a reasonable basis for our findings and conclusions based on our audit objectives. We believe that the evidence obtained provides a reasonable basis for our findings and conclusions based on our audit objectives. Appendix I provides a detailed description of our objectives, scope, and methodology.

RESULTS IN BRIEF

Several challenges have limited U.S. and international efforts to stabilize Somalia. The international community, including the United States, is seeking to improve the security situation in Somalia, mainly by funding an African Union peacekeeping operation. However, given the operation's shortage of troops, it has not been able to fulfill its mandate to improve security, support reconciliation, protect the transitional government, and facilitate the provision of humanitarian aid. In addition, the most recent attempt at national political reconciliation was limited, in part because several important opposition groups were not involved. For example, while this key attempt resulted in resolutions to end the conflict and return all property to its rightful owners, these opposition groups denounced the resolutions, citing their lack of participation in drafting them. Finally, according to many officials, Somalia's Transitional Federal Government lacks institutional structures and national acceptance, and these weaknesses have constrained U.S. and international efforts to establish it as a fully functioning central government. To mitigate these challenges, the international community, including the United States, is taking steps that include encouraging all parties to participate in reconciliation discussions.

While the international community, including the United States, continues to provide essential humanitarian and development assistance to Somalia, its efforts are limited by lack of security, sustained access to vulnerable populations, local implementing capacity, and effective government institutions. The international community's humanitarian assistance to Somalia, which primarily consists of food aid, has not reduced the country's acute malnutrition rates, which remain above the emergency threshold in some parts of the country. According to UN officials, however, malnutrition is the result of a combination of immediate and underlying causes, including insufficient dietary intake, inadequate health care, and inadequate water and sanitation services. Ongoing insecurity constrains the international community's ability to monitor and evaluate the effect of its humanitarian and development assistance to Somalia. Furthermore, U.S. officials' inability to travel to the country has prevented them from independently monitoring assistance. Finally, while the international community has pledged increased development assistance to Somalia, including to the south-central region, much of that assistance is conditioned on political progress and stability that have not yet been achieved.

The strategic planning effort to guide U.S. activities related to Somalia is incomplete. Although the Comprehensive Strategy generally addresses the components required of it by U.S. law, it does not cover the full range of U.S. government activities related to Somalia, such as DOD activities in the region intended to prevent conflict and promote stability. In addition, the strategy does not reference other documents that further elaborate on U.S. strategy and activities to achieve U.S. objectives in Somalia. For example, the Comprehensive Strategy does not mention USAID's 2006-2008 Strategy Statement for Somalia, which provides an assessment of the country's operating environment and discusses relevant strategic issues. Moreover, the Comprehensive Strategy does not fully address any of the six desirable characteristics of an effective national strategy, lacking such key elements as information on resources, risk management, and performance measures.

We recommend that the Secretary of State, in conjunction with the Secretary of Defense and the National Security Advisor, develop a more detailed U.S. strategy for Somalia, including the full range of U.S. government activities in the region and all six characteristics of an effective national strategy, in order to better inform Congress of U.S. policy and activities in the Horn of Africa.

DOD provided comments on a draft of our report, which we have reprinted in appendix IV. DOD partially concurred with our recommendation, suggesting that we strengthen our recommendation by calling for a "detailed U.S. strategy for Somalia," rather than a "more detailed report on U.S. strategy for Somalia." We have modified our report to recommend the development of a "*more* detailed strategy for Somalia," because we report that a governmentwide strategy for Somalia already exists. In a classified letter, State did not directly respond to our recommendation.[2] State's letter also included technical comments on this report, which we have incorporated as appropriate. Additionally, DOD, USAID, NSC, the World Bank, and various UN programs and offices provided technical comments and updated information, which we have included throughout this report as appropriate.

BACKGROUND

Somalia has lacked a functioning central government since 1991 and has experienced chronic humanitarian emergencies along with widespread and large-scale conflict. At least 15 national reconciliation conferences have been convened since 1991 to resolve Somalis' political differences and establish a central government. Because of insecurity in Somalia, the United States closed its embassy in Mogadishu in 1991 and has managed relations with Somalia from the U.S. embassy in Nairobi, Kenya.

CHRONIC HUMANITARIAN EMERGENCIES PLAGUE SOMALIA

Somalia is prone to chronic humanitarian emergencies produced by natural and man-made disasters and has been the site of continuous humanitarian operations since 1990. The UN and the World Bank classify Somalia as a least-developed, low-income country and one of the most food-insecure countries in the world.[3] Somalis have suffered from persistent high levels of poverty, and Somalia's human development indicators are among the lowest in the world. For example, according to the UN's 2006 Human Development Report, life expectancy at birth is only 46 years and only 29 percent of the population has access to a source of clean water. According to the UN, recent data suggest that the under-5 mortality rate is 135 per 1,000 births. Somalia currently has a population of about 8.8 million, according to State, of which roughly 1 million are considered internally displaced, having been forced or obliged to leave their homes to avoid conflict without crossing an internationally recognized border.

POLITICAL CONTEXT MARKED BY CONFLICT AND INSECURITY

Somalia's recent history has been marked by long periods of dictatorship or instability. The former British Protectorate of Somaliland and the former Italian-administered UN trust territory of Somalia gained independence in 1960 and united to form the Republic of Somalia. Somalia democratically elected its first president in 1960. Less than a decade later, Major General Mohamed Siad Barre's regime overthrew the government and imposed a dictatorship that lasted until 1991, when armed opposition groups drove Barre out of power and caused the collapse of the central government. The absence of a central government, combined with the impact of droughts, contributed to a series of humanitarian crises during the 1990s. In April 1992, the UN launched the UN Operation in Somalia, a peacekeeping operation aimed at providing security for humanitarian relief efforts. In December 1992, after the situation in Somalia further deteriorated, the United States launched a peace enforcement operation in Somalia aimed at establishing a secure environment for humanitarian relief operations. That mission, the U.S.-led Unified Task Force on Somalia, imposed a cease-fire and facilitated the delivery of humanitarian aid. A second UN operation in Somalia succeeded the Unified Task Force in May 1993 and was charged with the task of restoring peace, stability, law, and order in Somalia through disarmament and reconciliation. From 1993 to 1995, UN peacekeeping forces were drawn into a difficult and protracted conflict with Somali warlords. After 18 U.S. Army Rangers and hundreds of Somalis were killed in fierce fighting on October 3, 1993, the United States announced the withdrawal of its forces by March 1994. When the last UN forces withdrew, in March 1995, Somalia remained divided by warring factions and without a central government.

In the absence of a national government, Somalia has struggled to remain unified. In May 1991, northwestern Somalia unilaterally declared independence as the Republic of Somaliland (see fig. 1). Somaliland's claim to independence as a sovereign nation-state has not gained international recognition. In August 1998, the Puntland State of Somalia was formed as an autonomous, self-governing entity in the northeastern region with the long-term goal of being part of a federated Somalia. Unlike south-central Somalia, the northern regions of Somaliland and Puntland have managed to limit violence, establish democratic systems and institutions, and provide some basic services.

Source: GAO from UN map.

Disclaimer: The boundaries and names shown and the designations used on this map do not imply official endorsement or acceptance by the United Nations.

Note: A boundary dispute between Somaliland and Puntland remains unresolved.

Figure 1. Somalia.

EFFORTS TO ESTABLISH A CENTRAL GOVERNMENT CONTINUE

At least 15 national reconciliation conferences have been convened since 1991. In 2000, a major reconciliation conference in Djibouti (the 13th such effort) led to the formation of a new national government, the Transitional National Government, but this government was unable to establish itself as an effective administration beyond parts of Mogadishu, and its 3-year mandate expired in August 2003. In 2002, the Intergovernmental Authority on Development, a regional East African organization, organized a subsequent national reconciliation conference in Kenya. The conference concluded in 2004 with the formation of an interim government—the TFG[4]—including an interim President, Prime Minister, and cabinet. The Transitional Federal Charter was approved in February 2004, following the 2002-2004 national reconciliation conference, and provided a temporary legal underpinning for the Somali state and a framework for the transitional political process. The charter called for the drafting of a new constitution, a national referendum on this constitution, and the undertaking of a national census. The TFG has a 5-year mandate that expires in 2009 and is supposed to lead to national elections for the establishment of a permanent government.

Because of insecurity, the TFG was unable to establish itself in Mogadishu and instead based itself first in Jowhar and then in the southeastern town of Baidoa, where it eventually convened the transitional parliament in February 2006. The UN Monitoring Group on Somalia reported that in early 2006, a third party provided financial support to help organize and structure a militia force, known as the Alliance for the Restoration of Peace and Counter Terrorism (the Alliance), to counter the threat posed by the growing militant fundamentalist movement in south-central Somalia.[5] The Alliance and the Council of Islamic Courts[6]—a loose coalition of clerics, business leaders, and Islamic court militias—struggled for control of Mogadishu during the first half of 2006. The Islamic Courts defeated the Alliance in June 2006. With the TFG in command of little more than the government seat of Baidoa and warlords controlling much of southern Somalia, the Islamic Courts took control of Mogadishu. As its power in the south expanded, the Islamic Courts began to confront the TFG in Baidoa, and international efforts to broker an agreement between the two parties failed.

In December 2006, Ethiopian troops intervened forcefully on the side of the TFG, routing the Islamic Courts in Mogadishu and enabling the TFG to start establishing itself there. In January 2007, DOD carried out two military air strikes against al Qaeda affiliates in Somalia. The Director of National Intelligence reported that while the Ethiopian intervention disrupted al Qaeda's operations in the region, senior al Qaeda operatives responsible for the 1998 U.S. embassy bombings in Nairobi, Kenya, and Dar es Salaam, Tanzania, and the 2002 attacks in Mombasa, Kenya, remain at large as of February 2008. While some officials in the international community have accused the Islamic Courts of linkages with terrorist organizations and pursuing a policy of aggressive expansionism, NGOs and UN agencies have said, during the Islamic Courts' 6-month rule, there was general security and they had better access to project sites. As of February 2008, Ethiopian troops remain in Somalia while the TFG struggles to overcome internal divisions and establish its authority. In October 2007, facing a vote of confidence in the Transitional Federal Parliament, the Prime Minister of the TFG resigned. One month later, Somalia's Parliament swore in a new Prime Minister.

U.S. GOVERNMENT HAS NO OFFICIAL REPRESENTATION IN SOMALIA

The United States, like most of the international community, has managed its diplomatic and programmatic activities for Somalia from Nairobi, Kenya. Although the United States never formally severed diplomatic relations with Somalia, the U.S. embassy in Somalia has been closed since the collapse of the government in 1991. The United States maintains regular dialogue with the TFG and other key stakeholders in Somalia through the U.S. embassy in Nairobi. Because of security concerns, U.S. government officials face stringent restrictions on traveling to Somalia that they do not face elsewhere.

SEVERAL CHALLENGES HAVE LIMITED U.S. AND INTERNATIONAL EFFORTS TO STABILIZE SOMALIA

Several challenges have limited U.S. and international efforts to stabilize Somalia. The international community is seeking to improve the security situation in Somalia by funding an African Union peacekeeping operation and security sector reform programs, but a shortage of troops has hindered peacekeepers' ability to achieve their mission. In addition, attempts at political reconciliation, which have focused on the National Reconciliation Congress (NRC), have been limited by the lack of participation of all relevant Somali parties and the absence of a cease-fire or peace agreement. Finally, U.S. and international efforts to strengthen the central government, which have focused on capacity building, have been constrained by what many officials consider the TFG's lack of institutional structures and national acceptance.

EFFORTS TO IMPROVE SECURITY FOCUS ON PEACEKEEPING, BUT THEY ARE LIMITED BY SHORTAGE OF TROOPS

The international community's efforts to improve security in Somalia have focused on support for the African Union peacekeeping mission to Somalia (AMISOM), but the peacekeeping efforts have been hindered by a shortage of troops and the African Union's limited capacity to plan, command, and conduct operations effectively. The African Union authorized sending a peacekeeping mission of about 7,600 troops to Somalia for 6 months in January 2007 [7] and extended this mandate for an additional 6 months in July 2007. As of February 2008, Uganda and Burundi were the only countries contributing troops to AMISOM, with approximately 1,600 Ugandan and 800 Burundian troops in Somalia. The United States has provided roughly $60 million to support AMISOM, including funding to train and equip these troops. Additional funding from the international community will most likely be required to equip and deploy additional troops.

Despite international support, the mission has so far failed to reach the planned level of 7,600 troops. Potential troop-contributing countries have cited the shortage of funds and equipment, the lack of significant political reconciliation or cease-fire agreement, and Somalia's rapidly deteriorating security situation, especially in Mogadishu, as reasons for not contributing troops to the mission. Additionally, some U.S. and UN officials told us that many African nations are unable to provide any additional troops given their peacekeeping obligations in other countries, such as Sudan.

Given the limited number of troops deployed, AMISOM has not been able to fulfill its mandate to improve the security situation, support reconciliation, protect the transitional government, and facilitate the provision of humanitarian aid.[8] The Ugandan troops are facing considerable security challenges and have therefore limited their activities to patrolling only parts of Mogadishu and assisting in the provision of humanitarian assistance. According to a U.S. official, the Ugandans are limited to protecting only the airport, seaport, and presidential compound. U.S. and UN officials told us that the peacekeeping operation would likely be unable to achieve all of its objectives even if it were fully deployed with 7,600 troops, as the number is too low given the severity of the situation. In addition, these officials noted that, based on their assessments, the best-case scenario would require roughly 20,000 troops, as well as a cease-fire agreement and all parties' agreement to the mission. If these conditions are not met, more than 20,000 troops would most likely be needed. This assessment was based on the current situation as well as lessons learned from UN peacekeeping missions to Somalia in the 1990s that failed to achieve their objectives, although they involved 25,000 troops, including Americans, and what many experts consider better overall security conditions.

In August 2007, the UN Security Council passed a resolution that requested the Secretary-General of the UN to continue developing contingency planning for the possible deployment of a UN peacekeeping mission in Somalia that would replace the existing AMISOM. However, the UN Secretary-General said in November 2007 that under the prevailing conditions in Somalia, a peacekeeping operation is not a realistic and viable option. According to the UN Department of Peacekeeping Operations (UNDPKO), proper conditions include a cease-fire agreement and an invitation from all relevant parties, and the peacekeeping operation should be parallel with and in support of an inclusive political process leading toward reconciliation. Despite the UN Secretary-General's statement, the UN Security Council has continued to request more contingency planning by the UN. In March 2007, at the UN Security Council's request, UNDPKO conducted a technical assessment mission to develop contingency planning. Unlike typical assessment missions, this mission was somewhat less robust given the security situation in Somalia. For example, the mission involved fewer staff than a typical mission and was based in Nairobi and Addis Ababa, with only two short trips into Somalia—neither of which was to Mogadishu, as all attempts to go there were thwarted by violence both in the city and on the roads leading to it. Furthermore, UNDPKO was unable to conduct a planned second technical assessment mission in August 2007 because of heightened insecurity in Mogadishu. According to UN officials, UNDPKO conducted its second technical assessment mission in January 2008.

In addition to peacekeeping efforts, the international community is implementing other programs to improve the security situation in Somalia, including security sector reform and conflict mitigation. For example, the United Nations Development Program (UNDP) implements programs aimed at contributing to Somali efforts to restore a peaceful and secure environment that will promote social and economic recovery. These programs include efforts to establish a professional, accountable, and effective police service and support the TFG's review of the role and size of its security sector to facilitate the demobilization and reintegration of former combatants, militia, and retiring members of the formal security forces. In addition, DOD approved a transfer of $25 million to State in 2007 for security sector reform and other stabilization programs for Somalia.[9] This transfer includes $17.5 million for State and USAID programs aimed at security sector reform, peace and reconciliation, capacity building for the Transitional Federal Institutions, and quick-impact stabilization, and $7.5 million for USAID conflict mitigation programs in strategic border areas abutting Somalia in Kenya and Ethiopia.

DOD is also working to promote stability and prevent conflict in the Horn of Africa through the Combined Joint Task Force-Horn of Africa

(CJTF-HOA). For example, CJTF-HOA has implemented reconstruction and civil affairs projects in Kenya and Ethiopia in an effort to reduce support for extremist elements. In addition, DOD is working with neighboring countries to strengthen their counterterrorism capabilities through military-to-military training and foreign military financing.

LACK OF PARTICIPATION BY ALL SOMALI PARTIES HAS LIMITED EFFORTS TO PROMOTE RECONCILIATION

International attempts to support political reconciliation, which have focused on the NRC, have been limited by the lack of participation of all relevant Somali parties. The international community, including the United States, has provided broad support for the NRC since it was announced in early 2007. The international community provided $8 million through UNDP—including $2.25 million from the United States—to help organize the NRC and to promote the independence and strengthen the capacity of its oversight body, the National Governance and Reconciliation Committee. UNDP provided technical assistance and advice to the committee and promoted progress toward completion of essential tasks related to NRC implementation. UNDP also provided the committee with 14 staff members to assist in organizing the NRC, including 4 in Mogadishu, and administered the NRC budget. State, USAID, and a public affairs team from DOD operating at the U.S. embassy in Nairobi also helped promote participation in the NRC by funding radio messages and designing T-shirts, stickers, and banners (see fig. 2). In addition, USAID funded efforts to facilitate meetings between subclans of a key Somali clan and encouraged dialogue on the various concerns of many subclans about the NRC, in an attempt to achieve full clan participation at the congress. UN officials made periodic trips to Mogadishu to observe the congress, but U.S. officials did not, because of restrictions on their travel to Somalia.

Because several key Somali opposition groups did not participate in the NRC in July and August 2007, attempts to achieve political reconciliation through the NRC have been limited. The NRC was held in Mogadishu and comprised over 2,600 delegates representing the clans, women, and the diaspora, but some of the relevant parties to the ongoing conflict in Somalia did not attend, such as some of the key Somali subclans, as well as some opposition groups based outside the country. An observer of the situation in

Source: State.

Figure 2. U.S.-Designed T-Shirt Used to Build Support for the NRC.

Somalia noted that the opposition groups set the unrealistic precondition for attending the NRC of the withdrawal of Ethiopian troops from Somalia. The NRC resulted in agreements to end the conflict and return all property to itsrightful owners and called for a cease-fire amongst the clans, but opposition groups immediately denounced the agreements, citing their lack of participation in drafting them. Furthermore, according to UN officials, the NRC did not include any discussion of how to implement these agreements. In September 2007, a coalition of opposition groups met separately in Asmara, Eritrea, further diminishing the chances for political reconciliation among all Somali parties. Participants included representatives of the Islamic Courts, former members of the Somali Transitional Federal Parliament, members of the Somali diaspora, members of civil society, and clan elders. In its final communiqué from the conference, the Alliance for the Liberation and Reconstitution of Somalia stated its overriding aim was to liberate Somalia from Ethiopian occupation and launch a political reconstitution process that would involve all Somali stakeholders and rebuild a national state.

Since the NRC concluded in August 2007, the security situation in Somalia has not improved. The situation in Mogadishu has remained volatile, with daily attacks by insurgents targeting TFG forces and Ethiopian military personnel. The international community has shifted its focus to the transition process as outlined in the Transitional Federal Charter while continuing to search for ways to bring the relevant parties together. UN Department of Political Affairs officials told us that the entire international community must work to further advance the political process, by taking actions that include creating a platform to bring the two competing reconciliation processes together and involving Somalis not included in those two groups. Participants at a September 2007 donors meeting determined that in order to fulfill the provisions of the transitional charter, the TFG needs a road map with elements such as an inclusive process to shape the permanent constitution, a referendum on the constitution, and preparations for elections, including a census. The donors also agreed that the international community should be more assertive in reaching out to the opposition and mediating its participation in an inclusive and genuine national reconciliation process. In particular, officials from the UN and donors we spoke with, including the United States, said that the UN Political Office for Somalia (UNPOS) needed to take on a stronger leadership role in encouraging the government to be inclusive. According to UN officials, the UN Secretary-General's appointment in September 2007 of a new Special Representative for Somalia to oversee UNPOS showed that UNPOS was in fact taking on this more active role. UNPOS officials cautioned, however, that UNPOS's role is only that of an adviser and it is ultimately up to the TFG leaders to truly engage with the opposition parties.

WEAKNESS OF TRANSITIONAL GOVERNMENT HAS HINDERED INTERNATIONAL EFFORTS TO BUILD ITS CAPACITY AND CREATE A FUNCTIONING CENTRAL GOVERNMENT

The international community's efforts to support the establishment of the TFG as a fully functioning central government have been constrained by the TFG's lack of institutional structures, as well as the absence of widespread support for the TFG by the Somali people. According to several

U.S. and UN officials, the Transitional Federal Institutions, the underlying governance structures of the TFG, are not yet functioning, have almost no civil service staff, and lack the capacity to provide much-needed basic services to the Somali population. In addition, the TFG's lack of police and military forces hinders its ability to maintain security in Somalia. UN officials have reported that working with the TFG is often difficult, as most of its ministries exist in name only, with no support staff. For example, the TFG said after two meetings that it was not ready to participate in a committee through which donors were attempting to engage it in the prioritization and coordination of activities in Somalia, as it was still establishing itself and most of its ministries consisted only of an acting minister. Furthermore, some Somalia observers view the TFG as a narrow political and clan coalition rather than as an inclusive government of national unity. The Somaliland government, for example, considers itself wholly autonomous of the TFG. Moreover, an armed insurgency has continually staged attacks against the TFG, further hindering its ability to effectively govern Somalia.

Despite these challenges, the international community has taken steps to help the TFG become a fully functioning central government. The UN, with funding from the international community, and the United States have implemented programs in Somalia aimed at building the TFG's governance capacity and credibility. UNDP has funded the construction of many of the government buildings in Baidoa and is providing technical assistance to the TFG. It has facilitated the deployment of experts from the diaspora, such as economists and legal advisers, to assist the President, Prime Minister, and Speaker of Parliament in their duties. In addition, UNDP has provided support for administration reform to three civil service commissions. The United States is also conducting activities aimed at strengthening the capacity of the TFG's governing institutions and increasing its ability to provide basic social services. To support these activities, in May 2007, the Secretary of State appointed a Special Envoy for Somalia to represent the United States to the TFG. State has also increased the number of staff in the Somalia Unit at the U.S. embassy in Nairobi from one in December 2006 to six as of February 2008.

The United States' efforts to support the establishment of a functioning central government in Somalia are further constrained by the lack of U.S. presence in Somalia. State Department officials in Nairobi have said that the lack of presence prevents them from effectively engaging with the TFG, as they must rely on telephone conversations rather than face-to-face meetings, which occur only when Somali government leaders visit Nairobi. Despite this limitation, State looked for ways to increase its political engagement with the TFG in 2007. For example, in April 2007, the Assistant Secretary of State for African Affairs visited Baidoa; this was the first visit to Somalia by a senior U.S. official in over a decade. While there, the Assistant Secretary met with TFG officials to express support for national reconciliation efforts and urge TFG leaders to reach out to key stakeholders in Mogadishu to prevent further violence. More recently, in December 2007, the Secretary of State met with the prime ministers of Somalia and Ethiopia and foreign ministers from the region in Ethiopia to discuss the situation in Somalia. At this meeting, she stressed the urgency of timely deployment of additional AMISOM contingents and the U.S. commitment to a regional approach to resolving the crises in Somalia and encouraged the Prime Minister of Somalia to facilitate the delivery of humanitarian assistance.

INSECURITY AND OTHER CHALLENGES HAVE LIMITED THE INTERNATIONAL COMMUNITY'S EFFORTS TO PROVIDE HUMANITARIAN AND DEVELOPMENT ASSISTANCE TO SOMALIA

The international community's efforts to provide humanitarian and development assistance to Somalia have been limited by numerous challenges, including lack of security, sustained access to vulnerable populations, local implementing capacity, and effective government institutions. The international community's humanitarian assistance to Somalia, which primarily consists of food aid, has not reduced the country's acute malnutrition rates. These rates remain above the emergency threshold in some parts of the country. Ongoing insecurity constrains the international community's ability to monitor its provision of humanitarian and development assistance to Somalia. U.S. officials have not been able to independently monitor assistance because they have not been able to travel to Somalia. The international community's plans to provide increased development assistance to Somalia hinge on political progress and stability, which have not yet been achieved.

Donors Have Primarily Funded Food Aid to Somalia; Malnutrition Rates Remain above Emergency Threshold

According to UN data, the international community, including the United States, provided at least $1 billion in humanitarian assistance to Somalia from 2001 through 2007.[10] This included $745 million in assistance through the UN's annual appeals for funding to support humanitarian needs in Somalia from 2001 through 2007, of which roughly 47 percent, or $349 million, was for food aid.[11] Through the consolidated appeals, donors have funded a greater percentage of UN-estimated requirements for food aid than for any other individual sector.

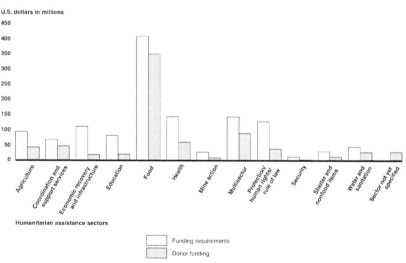

Source: GAO analysis of OCHA data.

Note: Requirements represent the total value of all projects proposed by implementing partners through the UN's consolidated appeal for Somalia for each sector. Funding reflects contributions by donors or agencies as a result of the appeals. If a donor makes a contribution to the UN's annual appeals, but does not specify project and sector, the UN attributes the funds to "sector not yet specified."

Figure 3. Funding Requirements and Donor Funding by Sector for Humanitarian Assistance to Somalia through the UN Consolidated Appeals Process for Fiscal Years 2001 through 2007.

As figure 3 shows, from 2001 through 2007, donors funded consolidated food aid appeals at an average level of 86 percent of these estimated requirements, while all other sectors combined were funded at an average level of 45 percent.

The UN has stressed the need for more balanced funding among the humanitarian sectors. According to UN officials, donors have typically funded stand-alone, short-term, visible interventions in Somalia, such as emergency food aid, rather than integrated, long-term, sustainable interventions.[12] UN and U.S. officials said that while they recognize the need to reduce the country's food insecurity by focusing more on other sectors besides food aid, such as agriculture and livelihoods, Somalia's constant state of crisis necessitates an emergency response.[13] Therefore, food aid and other humanitarian assistance to Somalia are primarily aimed at the immediate need to save lives rather than the improvement of livelihoods in the mid- to long term. Furthermore, donors have been reluctant to fully fund all humanitarian assistance sectors because of concerns that implementing partners in Somalia do not have the operational capacity or human resources to effectively use additional funding, as well as a desire for increased stability in Somalia before they provide additional funding.

The United States is the largest government donor of humanitarian assistance, including food aid, to Somalia. From fiscal years 2001 through 2007, the United States provided over $317 million in humanitarian assistance to Somalia through USAID and State (see fig. 4), with agencies and offices contributing as follows:[14]

- $242 million in food aid in the form of commodities from USAID's Office of Food for Peace, to the UN World Food Program (WFP) and CARE;
- $53 million from USAID's Office of Foreign Disaster Assistance to UN agencies and NGOs, to support a range of nonfood aid, such as logistics, nutrition, health, water, sanitation, and hygiene programs;
- $22 million from State's Bureau of Population, Refugees, and Migration to UN agencies, the International Committee of the Red Cross, and NGOs, to provide assistance to conflict-affected populations, including internally displaced persons (IDP), in Somalia.[15]

Somali Refugees in Dadaab, Kenya

Since 1991, the United Nations High Commissioner for Refugees (UNHCR) has managed a refugee camp in the town of Dadaab, Kenya, which is 80 kilometers from the Kenya/Somali border. Currently, the camp is home to over 173,000 refugees, nearly all of whom are Somali. UNHCR is responsible for the protection of and provision of assistance to refugees in coordination with its implementing partners—the Kenyan government, UN agencies, and NGOs. UN agencies and NGOs provide humanitarian assistance, such as food, water and sanitation, shelter, health care, and education to the refugees. The Kenyan government maintains a strict encampment policy that confines refugees to the camps because local integration is not considered a durable solution. Although the Somali border with Kenya remains officially closed, UNHCR officials told us that the camp received over 8,500 arrivals from Somalia from January to July 2007. Like Somalia, Dadaab has recently received increased international attention, which has raised the number of implementing and operational partners working in the camp from 4 in 2006 to 12 in 2007.

U.S. Commodities at Storage Facility

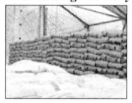

Shelter for Refugees

Source: GAO.

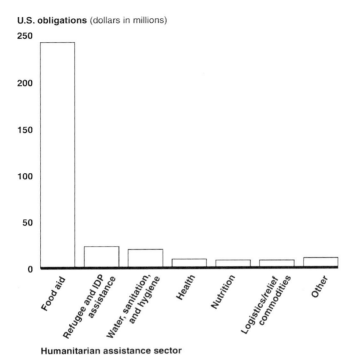

Source: GAO analysis of State and USAID data.
Notes:
"Logistics/relief commodities" include nonfood relief commodities, logistics, transportation, and air support. "Other sectors" includes agriculture and food security, economy and market systems, protection, coordination, stockpile, administrative support, travel, capacity building, research studies, shelter and settlements, and disaster support programs.
"Refugee and IDP assistance" represent funding from State's Bureau of Population, Refugees, and Migration. In addition to this funding, USAID's Offices of Foreign Disaster Assistance and Food for Peace also often provide a large percentage of their assistance to IDPs.

Figure 4. U.S. Humanitarian Assistance for Somalia in Fiscal Years 2001 through 2007 by Sector.

While donors have funded food aid at high levels, acute malnutrition rates in Somalia have remained chronically above the emergency threshold. According to data provided by the UN's Food and Agriculture Organization's Food Security Analysis Unit,[16] from 2001 through 2007, the mean prevalence rate of global acute malnutrition throughout Somalia was 15.6 percent—above the emergency threshold of 15 percent.[17] During this period, global acute malnutrition rates were higher in south-central

Somalia, at 17.3 percent, than in Somaliland and Puntland, which have a 12.5 and 11.7 percent malnutrition rate, respectively. In some regions in south-central Somalia, acute malnutrition rates have exceeded 20 percent. The UN estimates that 83,000 children are acutely malnourished in south-central Somalia, a figure that excludes IDPs, whose malnutrition rates are often higher. According to the Food Security Analysis Unit, malnutrition results from a complex set of elements, including high incidence of disease, lack of sanitation facilities and potable water, limited health services, and inappropriate child care practices. U.S. and UN officials told us that food aid by itself does not address the underlying causes of malnutrition in Somalia and the international community needs to implement a coordinated approach that integrates interventions in various sectors, such as water, health, and sanitation, to improve the nutritional situation in the country.

INSECURITY AND RELATED CHALLENGES HAVE HINDERED INTERNATIONAL HUMANITARIAN AID EFFORTS AND OVERSIGHT

Insecurity

Ongoing insecurity has been the most significant obstacle to the provision and oversight of humanitarian assistance in Somalia. Insecurity affects all aspects of the delivery of assistance to the country and prevents most UN international staff, international NGO staff, and donors from maintaining a permanent presence there, hindering assistance efforts and reducing monitoring capacity. The international community manages its assistance to Somalia by "remote control" from Nairobi through numerous working groups. Some UN officials told us that the coordination meetings on Somalia that occur in Nairobi consist mainly of information sharing and are burdensome and time-consuming. These officials also told us there is a need for more coordination to occur in Somalia rather than in Nairobi. UN agencies' and international NGOs' programs for Somalia are mainly implemented by Somali national staff, often without the on-site technical support, guidance, and authority of international program managers who remain in Kenya.

Although humanitarian needs are greater in south-central than in northern Somalia, because of ongoing insecurity, the international community generally has less access to south-central Somalia, especially Mogadishu, than to the northern regions (see fig. 5).

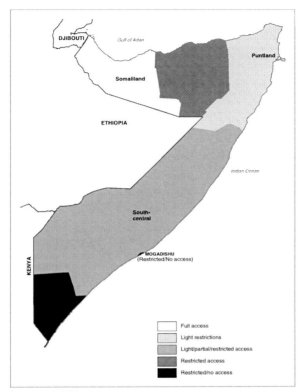

Source: GAO from UN OCHA.

Disclaimer: The boundaries and names shown and the designations used on this map do not imply official endorsement or acceptance by the United Nations.

Notes:

1. The UN security phases in effect in Somalia are indicative of the security situation there. Mogadishu is in phase five (evacuation of all United Nations staff), and the remainder of Somalia is in phase four (emergency operations only), except for the western part of Somaliland, which is in phase three.

2. Full access: no restrictions on humanitarian activity in the area and unimpeded ability to reach vulnerable populations.

Light restrictions: some interruptions on humanitarian activity and some constraints in reaching vulnerable populations.

Light/partial/restricted access: significant interruptions in humanitarian activity and significant constraints in reaching vulnerable populations.

Restricted access: seriously constrained humanitarian activity and minimal ability to reach vulnerable populations.

Restricted/no access: ongoing restrictions that prevent any humanitarian activity in the area.

3. A boundary dispute between Somaliland and Puntland over the Sool and Sanaag regions remains unresolved. On the map, these disputed regions are designated as restricted access.

Figure 5. International Community's Level of Access to Somalia.

The insecure operating environment in Somalia has led to breaks and delays in the delivery of humanitarian aid, thereby affecting human survival. For example, insecurity has limited the international community's ability to provide humanitarian assistance to 230,000 IDPs living in desperate conditions along a road between Mogadishu and Afgooye and lacking access to urgently needed food, clean water, sanitation, and health care. Delivery of humanitarian aid to vulnerable populations has not been possible or has been interrupted when the safety and security of humanitarian aid workers could not be ensured. Humanitarian aid workers in Somalia have experienced harassment, arbitrary detention at key checkpoints, kidnapping, arrest, and attacks and have at times been completely prevented from conducting aid operations. In October 2007, for example, the WFP temporarily suspended its food distributions when TFG soldiers violated the UN premises in Mogadishu and arrested the program's Head of Office. The official was released 5 days later, and food aid and all other UN planned activities subsequently resumed.

Insecurity in Somalia has also limited the international community's efforts to monitor and evaluate the provision of humanitarian aid. Because of security concerns, U.S. government officials have been unable to travel to Somalia to monitor and evaluate U.S. assistance to the country. The last time USAID officials visited Somalia was in January 2006, when two officials visited Puntland. USAID and State officials we met with said they must rely on the reports produced by their implementing partners and are unable to travel to Somalia to verify the reports and assess the effectiveness of their programs. According to USAID officials, Somalia is one of the few countries in which USAID cannot independently monitor the humanitarian aid provided. Monitoring and evaluation are necessary to determine whether interventions have been implemented as expected, if they need to be changed, and whether they have been effective.

Lack of Access

Not only does it lack access to Somalia because of ongoing insecurity, the international community also faces logistical challenges in transporting humanitarian aid to vulnerable populations. UN agencies and NGOs told us that their lack of physical access to Somalia by sea, overland, and by air has created major delays and increased the cost of transporting supplies to the country. According to the UN, nearly 80 percent of food aid to Somalia by WFP is shipped by sea, but the availability of shippers willing to carry food to the country has been reduced by half because of concerns about piracy. At least 15 hijackings of ships off the coast of Somalia took place in 2007, with 3 of the attacks involving WFP-chartered ships. In August 2007, the UN Security Council passed a resolution encouraging member states to take appropriate action—consistent with international law—to protect merchant shipping, particularly the transport of humanitarian aid. Subsequently, in November 2007, French Navy vessels escorted two WFP ships. When the Kenyan government closed its border with Somalia in January 2007, UN agencies and NGOs had difficulty transporting humanitarian supplies into Somalia and reloading trucks from Somalia with supplies in Kenya. Relief convoys eventually received permission to cross the border into Somalia, but inconsistent authorization and delays hindered travel through July 2007. Once in Somalia, humanitarian relief items are frequently subject to arbitrary taxation and customs fees at TFG checkpoints and at ad hoc roadblocks manned by armed militias. In 2007, the UN received reports of TFG-manned checkpoints demanding that passing traffic—including humanitarian convoys—pay fees ranging from $20 to $133, and later up to $520, per truck. The closure of key airstrips in south-central Somalia during the first half of 2007 often prevented aid staff from reaching the country, and access has been further complicated by poor road, sea, and air infrastructure and flooding.

Limited Capacity

The limited implementing capacity of local NGOs in Somalia also constrains the delivery of humanitarian aid. UN agencies and international NGOs work through local Somali NGOs to implement their programs, but many of these local NGOs lack operational capacity, qualified staff, and technical expertise, and U.S. and UN officials we met with said there is a need to build their capacity to provide aid. In addition, NGO managers told us that the Somali staff they have trained often leave to work for the UN, further weakening the capacity of the NGOs. U.S. officials also expressed concern that local NGOs lack the capacity to spend additional funds effectively. Furthermore, the complex working environment in south-central Somalia prohibits the rapid start-up of new NGOs in districts or regions without exhaustive negotiations with community leaders and local authorities.

Ineffective Government Institutions

The lack of effective government institutions, particularly in south-central Somalia, further hampers the implementation of humanitarian activities. The TFG lacks the capacity to coordinate humanitarian aid and sometimes hinders the provision of humanitarian aid in Somalia. For example, in March and April 2007, the TFG imposed restrictions on the delivery of humanitarian aid. The TFG restricted UN agencies to the use of TFG institutions as their sole implementing partner, restricted the use of airports for the delivery of aid, stated that research and data collection efforts without TFG approval were invalid, and halted distribution of food aid for unspecified inspections and approval by the TFG. Following international pressure, including engagement by the U.S. Ambassador to Kenya, the TFG removed these restrictions in late April 2007 and designated an Inter-Ministerial Committee, chaired by the Minister of Health, as the focal point on the coordination of humanitarian aid.

INCREASE IN INTERNATIONAL COMMUNITY'S DEVELOPMENT ASSISTANCE HINGES ON POLITICAL PROGRESS AND STABILITY IN SOMALIA

In addition to humanitarian assistance, the international community, including the United States, pledged at least $771 million in development assistance to Somalia from 2001 through 2006 and plans to increase this amount in the future.[18] However, plans for an increase in development assistance depend on political reconciliation and stability in Somalia, which have not yet been achieved. For example, implementation of the UN, World Bank, European Union, and Norway's transitional assistance plans for Somalia—based on the Reconstruction and Development Program (RDP), a 5-year national development plan that was the result of a joint UN and World Bank postconflict needs assessment—will depend on political and security conditions, existing implementation capacities, the willingness of most donors to participate in the RDP, and resource availability.[19] Sweden and Italy had planned to arrange an international donor conference in 2006 to raise funds to support the RDP, but World Bank and UN officials told us that such a conference had not yet occurred, because of the continued lack of political reconciliation and stability in Somalia. More recently, at a meeting in Sweden in September 2007 to coordinate their assistance strategies for

Somalia, donors including the United States, the UN, and the World Bank affirmed that the scope and effectiveness of their development assistance are contingent on reasonable stability in operating areas and genuine attempts at good governance at the country's federal, regional, and local levels.

Since 2001, the United States has increased its development assistance to Somalia and has targeted more of it to south-central Somalia to support the TFG. From fiscal years 2001 through 2007, the United States provided nearly $45 million in development assistance to Somalia through UNDP and NGOs in support of programs aimed at strengthening the capacity of civil society, supporting conflict mitigation, and increasing access to basic services. U.S. development assistance to Somalia grew from $3 million in fiscal year 2001 to over $17 million in fiscal year 2007. In fiscal years 2001 through 2003, about 90 percent of U.S. development assistance funds were targeted at Somaliland and Puntland. By contrast, in fiscal year 2007, the majority of these funds were targeted at south-central Somalia. In 2007, U.S. development assistance to Somalia was aimed at building the TFG's capacity to govern and deliver social services, such as education, water, and health, to increase its credibility among its constituencies.[20] This assistance also supported grassroots peace and reconciliation processes, conflict mitigation programs, civil society, education activities, and media outreach.

U.S. STRATEGIC PLANNING FOR SOMALIA IS INCOMPLETE

While the Administration's March 2007 Comprehensive Strategy generally includes all the components mandated by U.S. law, it is incomplete because it does not include the full range of U.S. government activities for Somalia and does not reference other U.S. government strategic planning documents for Somalia. Furthermore, the Comprehensive Strategy does not address the six characteristics of an effective national strategy, which, in our view, enhance a strategy's usefulness in resource and policy decisions and better ensure accountability. [21] Several officials told us that U.S. strategy for Somalia comprises three separate documents. Our analysis shows that these strategies, considered together, provide more detail on important elements, such as costs and overall desired results, but still do not address all the characteristics of an effective national strategy.[22]

COMPREHENSIVE STRATEGY ADDRESSES LEGISLATION, BUT DOES NOT COVER FULL RANGE OF ACTIVITIES

The National Defense Authorization Act of Fiscal Year 2007 required the Comprehensive Strategy to include the following:

1. a clearly stated policy towards Somalia that will help establish a functional, legitimate, and unified national government in Somalia

that is capable of maintaining the rule of law and preventing Somalia from becoming a safe haven for terrorists;

2. a description of the type and form of bilateral, regional, and multilateral efforts to coordinate and strengthen diplomatic engagement with Somalia;

3. a description of an integrated political, humanitarian, intelligence, and military approach to counter transnational security threats in Somalia and throughout the countries of the Horn of Africa;

4. a description of an interagency framework involving the federal agencies and departments of the United States to plan, coordinate, and execute U.S. policy and activities in Somalia and throughout the countries of the Horn of Africa and to oversee policy and program implementation; and

5. guidance on the manner in which the comprehensive regional strategy will be implemented.

While the strategy submitted to Congress contains sections that generally address each of these requirements, it is incomplete in two ways. First, the strategy does not include all of the U.S. government activities mentioned earlier in this report, notably DOD efforts, although, according to a DOD official in Nairobi, DOD plays a role in each of the three U.S. strategic objectives for Somalia.[23] For example, although the strategy contains sections on security and stability and counterterrorism, it does not mention DOD efforts to prevent conflict and promote regional stability through CJTF-HOA. According to DOD officials, DOD maintains an official policy of "no boots on the ground" in Somalia. However, it conducts civil affairs projects, provides military-to-military training, delivers humanitarian assistance, and enhances disaster management capabilities in other countries in the Horn of Africa.

Second, the Comprehensive Strategy does not refer to other U.S. government strategic planning documents, which some officials consider part of the overall U.S. strategy for Somalia, nor do these other documents refer to the Comprehensive Strategy. For example, the Comprehensive Strategy does not mention USAID's Strategy Statement for 2006-2008, although the statement provides a detailed description of the country context and strategic issues that remained relatively constant as priority objectives evolved. Furthermore, the Comprehensive Strategy does not refer to agency planning documents, such as State's fiscal year 2007 Operational Plan for Somalia, which USAID officials said was a key document that discusses USAID's current and future strategy for Somalia, or the Mission

Performance/Mission Strategic Plans for Somalia or Kenya, which outline the intended goals, priority initiatives, and performance indicators with targets for the country team in Nairobi. In addition, while the Foreign Assistance Strategy for Somalia—which lays out a strategy and estimated funding requirements for fiscal years 2007 and 2008 to implement programs that advance U.S. interests in Somalia—refers to an "aggressive diplomatic strategy" and an "active public diplomacy approach," it does not refer specifically to the Comprehensive Strategy. State's report on the status of implementation of the Comprehensive Strategy, issued subsequent to the Foreign Assistance Strategy, does not mention other strategic documents, reflecting the lack of integration between the Comprehensive Strategy and other key planning documents.

Comprehensive Strategy Does Not Address the Characteristics of an Effective National Strategy

The Comprehensive Strategy does not fully address any of the six desirable characteristics of an effective national strategy that we have identified and used in our previous work, limiting its usefulness as a planning tool. While national strategies are not required by executive or legislative mandate to address a single, consistent set of characteristics, the six desirable characteristics, along with their underlying elements, are important because they help implementers effectively shape policies, programs, priorities, and resource allocations so that federal agencies and other stakeholders can achieve the desired results. We recognize that strategies are not end points, but dynamic working documents, and that implementation is the key to any strategic planning effort. The ultimate measure of the Comprehensive Strategy's value will be the extent to which it provides useful guidance for policy and decision makers in allocating resources and balancing priorities with other important objectives. Appendix II describes the six desirable characteristics of an effective national strategy in detail.

As shown in figure 6, the Comprehensive Strategy partially addresses five of the six characteristics and does not address one of them at all. The strategy addresses some elements related to its purpose, goals, and activities to achieve results but does not address other elements related to costs, risk management, and integration with relevant documents from other agencies. Appendix III provides more detail on our assessment of the Comprehensive Strategy.

Criteria	Comprehensive strategy
1. Clear purpose, scope, methodology	◕
2. Detailed discussion of problems, risks, and threats	◕
3. Desired goals, objectives, activities, and performance measures	◕
4. Description of resources, investments, and risk management	○
5. Delineation of U.S. government roles, responsibilities, and coordination mechanism	◕
6. Description of strategy's integration among and with other entities	◕

● Addresses
◕ Partially addresses
○ Does not address

Source: GAO analysis.

Note: The six characteristics can be subdivided into 27 separate elements for more detailed assessment. If the strategy addressed all of the elements related to a characteristic, we determined that it addressed this characteristic. If the strategy addressed at least one but not all of the elements related to a characteristic, we determined that it partially addressed this characteristic. If the strategy addressed none of the elements related to a characteristic, we determined that it did not address this characteristic.

Figure 6. Extent to Which the Comprehensive Regional Strategy on Somalia Addresses the Desirable Characteristics of an Effective National Strategy.

Our analysis found the following key weaknesses:

- *Purpose, scope, and methodology.* Although the Comprehensive Strategy clearly explains that it was written in response to a legislative mandate, it does not discuss the process through which it was produced and only partially addresses other elements related to its purpose, scope, and methodology. For example, it does not clearly state its purpose, and it does not explicitly discuss the assumptions that guided its development. A more complete description of these elements could make the strategy more useful to organizations responsible for its implementation and to oversight entities such as Congress.

- *Problem definition and risk assessment.* The strategy only partially describes the problems it is intended to address and the operating environment in which it will be implemented; for example, the strategy does not mention the severe restrictions on official U.S. travel to Somalia. Furthermore, the strategy includes no discussion of the causes of the problems it is intended to address or the quality of data available. A more detailed description of the problems and their causes would give the responsible parties better guidance on implementing the strategy.

- *Goals, objectives, activities, and performance measures.* The strategy clearly states that U.S. objectives in Somalia are to eliminate the terrorist threat, promote political stability, and respond to the humanitarian needs of the Somali people. The strategy also outlines priority initiatives and lists several activities intended to achieve these objectives. However, the discussion of performance measures and the process to monitor and report on progress is very limited; having these elements could enable more effective oversight and accountability. Without these elements, policy makers cannot effectively monitor the strategy's progress toward its stated goals. We acknowledge the existence of significant limitations on monitoring performance; for example, U.S. and UN officials in Nairobi repeatedly told us of the difficulties of traveling to Somalia to monitor and evaluate their programs. However, the strategy neither addresses these limitations nor describes plans to obtain better data.

- *Resources, investments, and risk management.* The strategy does not identify current or future costs of implementation, risk management principles, or resource allocation mechanisms. Guidance on determining costs and resources based on a risk management approach helps implementing parties allocate resources according to priorities, track costs and performance, and shift resources as appropriate. Risk management is especially important in planning for Somalia, where overall needs outweigh resources available because of the prolonged crisis.

- *Roles, responsibilities, and coordination.* The strategy generally indicates who will implement it, stating that "the Comprehensive Regional Strategy on Somalia will be implemented by the Department of State, in coordination with appropriate U.S. government agencies and departments," but it does not elaborate on the roles and responsibilities of agencies other than State, notably DOD. In addition, although the strategy identifies the Africa Policy Coordination Committee as the "interagency framework for planning, coordinating, and executing" U.S. policy in Somalia, it does not identify a process for resolving conflicts among agencies.[24]

- *Strategy's integration among and with other entities.* Although the strategy references other organizations, such as the International Contact Group on Somalia,[25] the UN, and the African Union, it does not address how it relates to these organizations' strategies or objectives for Somalia. Furthermore, as mentioned above, the strategy does not refer to other U.S. government strategic documents, such as the National Security Strategy or USAID's Strategy Statement for Somalia. However, the strategy does mention Somalia's Transitional Federal Charter and describes how efforts to promote political dialogue fit into the charter's framework. More information on how the strategy relates to these other documents would further clarify the relationships between various implementing partners within the U.S. government and the international community.

While the other documents that State and USAID officials consider part of the United States' overall strategy for Somalia provide more detail on certain elements within the six desirable characteristics of an effective strategy, they still do not fully address any of the characteristics. For example, the Foreign Assistance Strategy for Somalia provides significantly more detail on resource requirements, sources, and allocation mechanisms. In addition, USAID's Strategy Statement for Somalia includes a detailed discussion of the problems it is intended to address and the causes of these problems. However, none of these documents refer to the others, highlighting their lack of integration.

Our analysis of the joint UN-World Bank RDP—the international community's framework for development activities for Somalia—found that it does address the majority of elements of the six desirable characteristics, providing significantly more detail than the United States' Comprehensive Strategy. For example, the RDP clearly identifies its purpose, scope, and methodology; defines the problems it is intended to address and discusses the causes of these problems; addresses overall results, strategic goals, and activities; and identifies how much the strategy will cost and how resources should be targeted to balance risks and costs.

CONCLUSIONS

Enormous challenges have limited efforts to establish peace, stability, and a functioning central government in Somalia and to meet the Somalis' basic needs. Although State officials have encouraged African countries to contribute troops to the African Union peacekeeping mission in Somalia, the ongoing insurgency and lack of a peace agreement have limited AMISOM's ability to achieve its mission. State officials had hoped that a fully deployed AMISOM force would allow Ethiopian defense forces to withdraw from Somalia, which, in turn, would allow key nonviolent opposition groups to return to Somalia and participate in reconciliation efforts. To date, however, these groups and the transitional government have not engaged in any meaningful dialogue toward reconciliation. In addition, the transitional government's lack of institutional structures and national acceptance has hindered international activities to build governance capacity. Furthermore, insecurity, lack of access to Somalia, and other challenges have made it very difficult for humanitarian organizations to adequately address the needs of the country's most vulnerable populations—such as internally displaced persons—for food, water, housing, and health care. Addressing these challenges is critical, as Somalia will likely need humanitarian assistance for several years to come.

Moving Somalia toward the goal of national elections in 2009 will require sustained and concerted efforts from donors, international organizations, African nations, and, most important, Somalis themselves. The U.S. government has increased its political engagement with the Somali government and funding for assistance in Somalia, but the strategic planning effort to guide U.S. activities related to Somalia has been incomplete. As the

United States continues to formulate its role and respond to the volatile conditions in Somalia, a comprehensive strategy that fully addresses critical issues such as overall costs and monitoring and evaluation becomes increasingly important.

RECOMMENDATION FOR EXECUTIVE ACTION

In order to better inform Congress on U.S. policy and activities in Somalia and the Horn of Africa, we recommend that the Secretary of State, in conjunction with the Secretary of Defense and the National Security Advisor, develop a more detailed U.S. strategy for Somalia, including the full range of U.S. government activities in the region and all six elements of an effective national strategy.

APPENDIX I.
OBJECTIVES, SCOPE, AND
METHODOLOGY

In this report, we assess (1) U.S. and international efforts to stabilize Somalia; (2) U.S. and international efforts to provide humanitarian and development assistance to Somalia; and (3) strategic planning efforts to guide U.S. activities related to Somalia.

To assess U.S. efforts to stabilize Somalia and provide humanitarian and development assistance, we examined documents and interviewed officials from five U.S. government agencies in Washington, D.C.; New York; Nairobi, Kenya; and Addis Ababa, Ethiopia, about their activities for Somalia. Because of restrictions on official U.S. government travel to Somalia, we did not conduct fieldwork in the country. We reviewed various strategic, planning, budgetary, and reporting documents from these agencies outlining their ongoing activities for Somalia. At the State Department (State), we met with officials from the Bureaus of African Affairs, Diplomatic Security, and Population, Refugees, and Migration; the Offices of the Director of Foreign Assistance, the Undersecretary of Management, and the Coordinator for Reconstruction and Stabilization; and the U.S. missions to Kenya, Ethiopia, the United Nations, and the African Union. At the U.S. Agency for International Development (USAID), we met with officials from the Africa Bureau and the Offices of Foreign Disaster Assistance, Food for Peace, Transition Initiatives, and Conflict Management and Mitigation. At the Department of Defense (DOD) we met with officials from the Office of the Secretary of Defense, the Joint Chiefs of Staff, and the Combined Joint Task Force–Horn of Africa. We also met with experts on

Somalia from academia and the private sector, as well as numerous nongovernmental organizations implementing programs in Somalia, to discuss their views on U.S. activities related to Somalia.

To assess international assistance efforts for Somalia, we reviewed United Nations (UN) and World Bank reports, research, and strategic planning documents and met with officials in 10 UN offices and programs, the World Bank, nongovernmental organizations, the Somali government, and other donor governments. We conducted interviews with officials of the following UN entities: the Office for the Coordination of Humanitarian Affairs (OCHA), World Food Program, UN Development Program, UN Department of Safety and Security, UN Department of Political Affairs, UN Children's Fund, UN Department for Peacekeeping Operations, Food and Agriculture Organization, UN High Commissioner for Refugees (UNHCR), and World Health Organization. We also interviewed officials of the European Commission, the Arab League, the United Kingdom, and Italy. In Ethiopia, we met with officials of the African Union and the Ethiopian government. In addition, we traveled to a UNHCR camp in Dadaab, Kenya, to observe programs to assist Somali refugees. Finally, we attended several conferences whose attendees included representatives from the U.S. and Somali governments and Somali civil society organizations.

To determine U.S. funding for programs related to Somalia, we analyzed State, USAID, and DOD financial obligations for Somalia programs from fiscal years 2001 through 2007. We obtained data on U.S. humanitarian and development funding for this period, as well as the number of staff focused on programs relating to Somalia, from officials within State, USAID, and DOD. We assessed the reliability of these data by reviewing relevant existing information and interviewing cognizant agency officials, as well as by cross-checking the data we obtained from the agencies with other sources. We found all agencies' data sufficiently reliable for the purpose of our report, which was to show the large difference in U.S. funding between food aid and other humanitarian aid sectors, as well as development aid funding levels.

To determine the international community's funding for humanitarian assistance to Somalia from 2001 through 2007, we obtained data reported by OCHA's Financial Tracking Service (FTS) on both assistance provided in response to the UN's annual Consolidated Appeals Process (CAP) for Somalia from 2001 through 2007, as well as other humanitarian assistance provided (not in response to an appeal) from 2001 through 2007. To assess the reliability of these data, we discussed with OCHA officials their processes for receiving and compiling the information from donors and implementing partners and for ensuring fund totals are accurate and not double-counted.

In assessing the data from FTS on humanitarian funding through the CAP for Somalia, we found that firm reporting arrangements exist with implementing agencies that request funding through the CAP to ensure all funding received is reported. In particular, OCHA officials told us that the CAP funding data are tracked according to specific required project numbers and to related sector categories. The humanitarian funding through the CAP is therefore limited to funding for specific projects listed in the CAP, and is not trying to capture all assistance going to Somalia. We determined the funding information for the CAP to be reliable enough to provide as part of the total humanitarian assistance[1] provided to Somalia and as part of our evidence that food aid is funded at higher levels than other sectors in Somalia.

For humanitarian assistance reported to FTS for projects outside of the CAP, we found several limitations. OCHA officials and some Somalia experts told us that there are likely large amounts of humanitarian assistance being provided by some Gulf States that are not reported to the UN. Additionally, all donors may not report the full amount of assistance provided outside of the CAP (through FTS), and therefore it is possible for some donors' data to be incomplete. As a result, the figures we report here likely undercount total global humanitarian assistance. We found that despite these limitations, the data are reliable enough for reporting broadly on the minimum of total assistance provided, with the caveat that certain countries' data or portions of their data are excluded. Recognizing these limitations, we report a minimum funding total calculated by adding the CAP total to the total reported funding for humanitarian projects outside of the CAP.

We do not provide figures by sector for the data on funding provided for projects outside of the CAP because of possible inconsistencies and/or inaccuracies in how donors report the data to FTS. The UN provides guidance to donors on criteria for categorizing assistance by sector. However, OCHA officials told us that some donors use their own criteria rather than OCHA's. Additionally, we determined that because of the general nature of the guidance, countries may interpret the classifications of assistance that the UN provides differently. For these reasons we do not provide sector-specific figures for these data, but instead only report sector-specific data reported under the CAP.

To determine the international community's funding for development assistance to Somalia from 2001 through 2006, we obtained data from annual reports of the Somalia Aid Coordination Body (SACB), which consists of donors, UN agencies, and implementing partners active in Somalia. Through interviews and review of donor reports, we found that the Somali Support Secretariat,[2] which collects the data and issues the donor reports, attempts to ensure that assistance is counted only in one year and not recounted in subsequent years. However, a secretariat official told us that there is no extensive verification of information reported by donors, and there is little to no effort to include data on assistance provided by non-SACB donors, particularly those from the Middle East. We were only able to obtain data on development assistance through 2006 to provide a context for the level of development assistance pledged to Somalia over the past 6 years. Because of these limitations the amounts reported do not represent all development assistance to Somalia.

To assess the U.S. strategic planning efforts, we examined the Comprehensive Regional Strategy on Somalia (Comprehensive Strategy) and supporting documents and spoke with officials from State, USAID, DOD, and the National Security Council who were involved in the development of the Comprehensive Strategy. Officials from these agencies identified the following three documents, combined, as the United States' overall strategy for Somalia: the Comprehensive Strategy, the Foreign Assistance Strategy for Somalia for fiscal years 2007 and 2008, and USAID's Strategy Statement for Somalia (2006-2008). In addition to these documents, we reviewed other U.S. government documents that provide useful information though they were not identified as key supporting documents by State, USAID, or DOD officials. These documents include the Mission Performance Plan for the U.S. Mission to Kenya for fiscal years 2006, 2007, and 2008; the Mission Strategic Plan for the U.S. Mission to Somalia for fiscal year 2009; the fiscal year 2007 Operational Plan for Somalia; and the report on the status of implementation of the Comprehensive Strategy. We focused our analysis on the Comprehensive Strategy because it was the only one identified as a comprehensive, U.S. governmentwide strategy for Somalia and compared it against the components required of it by U.S. law.

To determine whether the Comprehensive Strategy contains all six desirable characteristics of an effective national strategy that we developed and used in our prior work, we first developed a checklist of these characteristics, along with their 27 component elements. (See app. II for a more detailed description of the six characteristics.) Three GAO staff members then independently assessed the Comprehensive Strategy for its inclusion of the 27 elements, recorded their findings on separate checklists, and met to reconcile any differences in their assessments. Once these assessments were reconciled, two additional GAO staff members reviewed this analysis for completeness and accuracy.

To determine the extent to which the Comprehensive Strategy addressed the six characteristics of an effective national strategy, we developed the following three categories: the strategy (1) addresses a characteristic when it explicitly cites all elements related to that characteristic; (2) partially addresses a characteristic when it explicitly cites at least one, but not all, of the elements related to that characteristic; and (3) does not address a characteristic when it does not explicitly cite any of the elements related to that characteristic. By applying these categories to our checklists of the 27 elements, we developed a consolidated summary of the extent to which the strategy addressed the six characteristics of an effective national strategy. We applied the same methodology to the Foreign Assistance Strategy and the USAID Strategy Statement to determine the extent to which these documents, combined with the Comprehensive Strategy, address these desirable characteristics. In addition, we applied this methodology to the joint UN-World Bank Reconstruction and Development Program to determine the extent to which it addresses the six characteristics.

We conducted this performance audit from January 2007 to February 2008 in accordance with generally accepted government auditing standards. Those standards require that we plan and perform the audit to obtain sufficient, appropriate evidence to provide a reasonable basis for our findings and conclusions based on our audit objectives. We believe that the evidence obtained provides a reasonable basis for our findings and conclusions based on our audit objectives.

APPENDIX II.
GAO'S DESCRIPTION OF THE SIX CHARACTERISTICS OF AN EFFECTIVE NATIONAL STRATEGY

In a prior report, we identified six desirable characteristics of an effective national strategy that would enable its implementers to effectively shape policies, programs, priorities, resource allocations, and standards and that would enable federal departments and other stakeholders to achieve the identified results.[1] We further determined in that report that national strategies with the six characteristics can provide policy makers and implementing agencies with a planning tool that can help ensure accountability and more effective results. To develop these six desirable characteristics of an effective national strategy, we reviewed several sources of information. First, we gathered statutory requirements pertaining to national strategies, as well as legislative and executive branch guidance. We also consulted the Government Performance and Results Act of 1993, general literature on strategic planning and performance, and guidance from the Office of Management and Budget on the President's Management Agenda. In addition, among other things, we studied past reports and testimonies for findings and recommendations pertaining to the desirable elements of a national strategy. Furthermore, we consulted widely within GAO to obtain updated information on strategic planning, integration across and between the government and its partners, implementation, and other related subjects. We developed these six desirable characteristics based on their underlying support in legislative or executive guidance and the frequency with which they were cited in other sources. We then grouped similar items together in a logical sequence, from conception to implementation. Table 1 provides these desirable characteristics and examples of their elements.

Table 1. Summary of Desirable Characteristics of an Effective National Strategy

Desirable characteristic	Brief description
Purpose, scope, and methodology	Addresses why the strategy was produced, the scope of its coverage, and the process by which it was developed.
Problems, risks, and threats	Addresses the particular national problems and threats the strategy is directed toward.
Desired goals, objectives, activities, and performance measures	Addresses what the strategy is trying to achieve; steps to achieve those results; as well as the priorities, milestones, and performance measures to gauge results.
Desirable characteristic	**Brief description**
Resources, investments, and risk management	Addresses what the strategy will cost, the sources and types of resources and investments needed, and where resources and investments should be targeted by balancing risk reductions and costs.
U.S. government roles, responsibilities, and coordination mechanism	Addresses who will be implementing the strategy, what their roles will be compared to those of others, and mechanisms for them to coordinate their efforts.
Integration among and with other entities	Addresses how a national strategy relates to other strategies' goals, objectives, and activities— and to subordinate levels of government and their plans to implement the strategy.

Source: GAO.

The following sections provide more detail on the six desirable characteristics.

PURPOSE, SCOPE, AND METHODOLOGY

This characteristic addresses why the strategy was produced, the scope of its coverage, and the process by which it was developed. For example, a strategy should discuss the specific impetus that led to its being written (or updated), such as statutory requirements, executive mandates, or other events like the Global War on Terrorism. Furthermore, a strategy would enhance clarity by including definitions of key, relevant terms. In addition to describing what it is meant to do and the major functions, mission areas, or activities it covers, a national strategy would ideally address its methodology. For example, a strategy should discuss the principles or theories that guided its development, the organizations or offices that drafted the document, or working groups that were consulted in its development.

PROBLEMS, RISKS, AND THREATS

This characteristic addresses the particular national problems and threats at which the strategy is directed. Specifically, this means a detailed discussion or definition of the problems the strategy intends to address, their causes, and operating environment. In addition, this characteristic entails a risk assessment, including an analysis of the threats to and vulnerabilities of critical assets and operations. If the details of these analyses are classified or preliminary, an unclassified version of the strategy should at least include a broad description of the analyses and stress the importance of risk assessment to implementing parties. A discussion of the quality of data available regarding this characteristic, such as known constraints or deficiencies, would also be useful.

GOALS, OBJECTIVES, ACTIVITIES, AND PERFORMANCE MEASURES

This characteristic addresses what the national strategy strives to achieve and the steps needed to garner those results, as well as the priorities, milestones, and performance measures to gauge results. At the highest level,

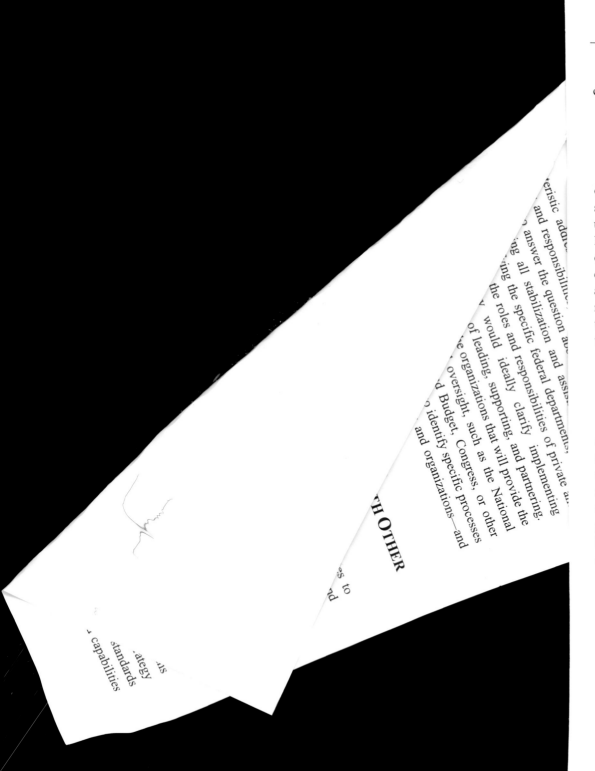

this could be a description of an ideal end state, followed
hierarchy of major goals, subordinate objectives, and speci'
achieve results. In addition, it would be helpful if the strate'
importance of implementing parties' efforts to est/
milestones, and performance measures, which help ensu
Ideally, a national strategy would set clear desired res
specific milestones, and outcome-related performance m
implementing parties flexibility to pursue and achieve
reasonable time frame. If significant limitations on '
exist, other parts of the strategy should address plans
measurements, such as national standards or indicate

RESOURCES, INVESTI
AND RISK MANAGE

This characteristic addresses what the str
types of resources and investments needed
investments should be targeted. Ideally,
appropriate mechanisms to allocate re'
strategy should elaborate on the risk ass
guidance to implementing parties to ma
accordingly. It should also address the
pays and how such efforts will be
Furthermore, a strategy should includ.
required, such as budgetary, human capita,
technology, research and development, procuremen
contract services. A national strategy should also discuss linkag.
resource documents, such as federal agency budgets or human capita
information technology, research and development, and acquisition
strategies. Finally, a national strategy should also discuss in greater detail
how risk management will aid implementing parties in prioritizing and
allocating resources, including how this approach will create societywide
benefits and balance these with the cost to society. Related to this, a national
strategy should discuss the economic principle of risk-adjusted return on
resources.

The following sections provide more detail on the six desirable characteristics.

PURPOSE, SCOPE, AND METHODOLOGY

This characteristic addresses why the strategy was produced, the scope of its coverage, and the process by which it was developed. For example, a strategy should discuss the specific impetus that led to its being written (or updated), such as statutory requirements, executive mandates, or other events like the Global War on Terrorism. Furthermore, a strategy would enhance clarity by including definitions of key, relevant terms. In addition to describing what it is meant to do and the major functions, mission areas, or activities it covers, a national strategy would ideally address its methodology. For example, a strategy should discuss the principles or theories that guided its development, the organizations or offices that drafted the document, or working groups that were consulted in its development.

PROBLEMS, RISKS, AND THREATS

This characteristic addresses the particular national problems and threats at which the strategy is directed. Specifically, this means a detailed discussion or definition of the problems the strategy intends to address, their causes, and operating environment. In addition, this characteristic entails a risk assessment, including an analysis of the threats to and vulnerabilities of critical assets and operations. If the details of these analyses are classified or preliminary, an unclassified version of the strategy should at least include a broad description of the analyses and stress the importance of risk assessment to implementing parties. A discussion of the quality of data available regarding this characteristic, such as known constraints or deficiencies, would also be useful.

GOALS, OBJECTIVES, ACTIVITIES, AND PERFORMANCE MEASURES

This characteristic addresses what the national strategy strives to achieve and the steps needed to garner those results, as well as the priorities, milestones, and performance measures to gauge results. At the highest level, this could be a description of an ideal end state, followed by a logical hierarchy of major goals, subordinate objectives, and specific activities to achieve results. In addition, it would be helpful if the strategy discussed the importance of implementing parties' efforts to establish priorities, milestones, and performance measures, which help ensure accountability. Ideally, a national strategy would set clear desired results and priorities, specific milestones, and outcome-related performance measures while giving implementing parties flexibility to pursue and achieve those results within a reasonable time frame. If significant limitations on performance measures exist, other parts of the strategy should address plans to obtain better data or measurements, such as national standards or indicators of preparedness.

RESOURCES, INVESTMENTS, AND RISK MANAGEMENT

This characteristic addresses what the strategy will cost, the sources and types of resources and investments needed, and where those resources and investments should be targeted. Ideally, a strategy would also identify appropriate mechanisms to allocate resources. Furthermore, a national strategy should elaborate on the risk assessment mentioned earlier and give guidance to implementing parties to manage their resources and investments accordingly. It should also address the difficult, but critical, issues about who pays and how such efforts will be funded and sustained in the future. Furthermore, a strategy should include a discussion of the type of resources required, such as budgetary, human capital, information, information technology, research and development, procurement of equipment, or contract services. A national strategy should also discuss linkages to other resource documents, such as federal agency budgets or human capital, information technology, research and development, and acquisition strategies. Finally, a national strategy should also discuss in greater detail how risk management will aid implementing parties in prioritizing and allocating resources, including how this approach will create societywide benefits and balance these with the cost to society. Related to this, a national strategy should discuss the economic principle of risk-adjusted return on resources.

U.S. GOVERNMENT ROLES, RESPONSIBILITIES, AND COORDINATION MECHANISM

This characteristic addresses what organizations will implement the strategy, their roles and responsibilities, and mechanisms for coordinating their efforts. It helps to answer the question about who is in charge during times of crisis and during all stabilization and assistance efforts. This characteristic entails identifying the specific federal departments, agencies, or offices involved, as well as the roles and responsibilities of private and international sectors. A strategy would ideally clarify implementing organizations' relationships in terms of leading, supporting, and partnering. In addition, a strategy should describe the organizations that will provide the overall framework for accountability and oversight, such as the National Security Council, Office of Management and Budget, Congress, or other organizations. Furthermore, a strategy should also identify specific processes for coordination and collaboration among sectors and organizations—and address how any conflicts would be resolved.

STRATEGY'S INTEGRATION AMONG AND WITH OTHER ENTITIES

This characteristic addresses both how a national strategy relates to other strategies' goals, objectives, and activities (horizontal integration) and how it relates to subordinate levels of government and other organizations and their plans to implement the strategy (vertical integration). For example, a national strategy should discuss how its scope complements, expands upon, or overlaps with other strategies prepared by other governments or international organizations. Similarly, related strategies should highlight their common or shared goals, subordinate objectives, and activities. In addition, a national strategy should address its relationship with relevant documents from implementing organizations, such as the strategic plans, annual performance plans, or the annual performance reports the Government Performance and Results Act requires of federal agencies. A strategy should also discuss, as appropriate, various strategies and plans produced by the state, local, private, and international sectors. A strategy also should provide guidance such as the development of national standards to link together more effectively the roles, responsibilities, and capabilities of the implementing parties.

APPENDIX III.
EXTENT TO WHICH THE COMPREHENSIVE REGIONAL STRATEGY ON SOMALIA ADDRESSES GAO'S DESIRABLE CHARACTERISTICS

We reviewed the content of the Comprehensive Regional Strategy on Somalia to determine the extent to which it addressed each of the six desirable characteristics of an effective national strategy that we previously developed and used in other contexts. (App. I explains our methodology in detail; app. II provides a detailed description of the six desirable characteristics.) We divided each characteristic into subelements for a more detailed assessment and then determined whether the Comprehensive Strategy addresses, partially addresses, or does not address each of the subelements and characteristics. Figure 7 shows the results of our assessment of the Comprehensive Strategy.

Characteristic	Section	Item
1. Clear purpose, scope, and methodology	◑	
Purpose		
1a. Identifies the impetus that led to the strategy being written, such as a statutory requirement, mandate, or key event.		●
1b. Discusses the strategy's purpose.		◑
Scope		
1c. Defines or discusses key terms, major functions, mission areas, or activities the strategy covers		●
Methodology		
1d. Discusses the process that produced the strategy, e.g., what organizations or offices drafted the document, whether it was the result of a working group, or which parties were consulted in its development.		○
1e. Discusses assumptions or the principles and theories that guided the strategy's development.		◑
2. Detailed discussion of problems, risks, and threats	◑	
Problem definition		
2a. Includes a detailed discussion or definition of the problems the strategy intends to address.		◑
2b. Includes a detailed discussion of the causes of the problems.		○
2c. Includes a detailed discussion of the operating environment.		◑
Risk Assessment		
2d. Addresses a detailed discussion of the threats at which the strategy is directed.		◑
2e. Discusses the quality of data available, e.g., constraints, deficiencies, and "unknowns."		○
3. Desired goals, objectives, activities, and outcome-related performance measures	◑	
Goals and subordinate objectives		
3a. Addresses the overall results desired, i.e., an "end state."		◑
3b. Identifies strategic goals and subordinate objectives.		●
Activities		
3c. Identifies specific activities to achieve results.		●
Performance measures		
3d. Addresses priorities, milestones, and outcome-related performance measures.		◑
3e. Identifies process to monitor and report on progress.		◑
3f. Identifies limitations on progress indicators.		○
4. Resources, investments, and risk management	◑	
Resources and investments		
4a. Identifies what the strategy will cost.		○
4b. Identifies the sources, e.g., federal, international, and private, and types of resources or investments needed, e.g., budgetary, human capital, information technology, research and development, and contracts.		○
Risk management		
4c. Addresses where resources or investments should be targeted to balance risks and costs.		○
4d. Addresses resource allocation mechanisms.		○
4e. Addresses risk management principles and how they help implementing parties prioritize and allocate resources.		○
5. Delineation of U.S. government roles, responsibilities, and coordination mechanism	◑	
Organizational roles and responsibilities		
5a. Addresses who will implement the strategy.		●
5b. Addresses lead, support, and partner roles and responsibilities of specific federal agencies, departments, or offices, e.g., who is in charge during all phases of the strategy's implementation.		◑
Coordination		
5c. Addresses mechanisms and/or processes for parties to coordinate efforts within agencies and with other agencies.		●
5d. Identifies process for resolving conflicts		○
6. Description of strategy's integration among and with other entities	◑	
6a. Addresses how the strategy relates to the strategies of other institutions and organizations' and their goals, ojectives, and activities (horizontal).		◑
6b. Addresses integration with relevant documents from other agencies and subordinate levels (vertical).		○

● Addresses
◑ Partially addresses
○ Does not address

Source: GAO analysis of State and USAID data.

Note: The strategy addresses a characteristic if it addresses all subelements of that characteristic. It partially addresses a characteristic if it partially addresses at least one subelement of that characteristic but does not address all subelements of that characteristic. It does not address a characteristic if it does not address any of the subelements of that characteristic.

Figure 7. Extent to Which the Comprehensive Regional Strategy on Somalia Addresses the 27 Elements of the Desirable Characteristics of a National Strategy.

REFERENCES

[1] John Warner National Defense Authorization Act of Fiscal Year 2007, Pub. L. 109-364, sec. 1226. This act called on the President to submit to Congress a report on a comprehensive regional strategy toward Somalia, including a clearly stated policy toward the country; a description of efforts to coordinate and strengthen diplomatic engagement; a description of an approach to counter transnational security threats in the region; a description of the interagency framework to plan, coordinate, and execute U.S. policy and activities in Somalia and in the region; and guidance on the manner in which the strategy will be implemented.

[2] State's letter is reprinted in our classified report.

[3] Food insecurity results from a lack of availability of food, from lack of access to food, and when food is not properly utilized.

[4] During the formation of the Transitional National Government, a template for power sharing based on fixed proportional representation by clan, known as the 4.5 formula, was established and then adopted again during the 2002-2004 talks that produced the Transitional Federal Government. Under this formula, Somalia's four major clans were allocated an equal number of seats in parliament and half that number was allocated to remaining minority groups. The four major clans are the Darood, Hawiye, Dir, and Digle-Mirifle.

[5] Somalia presents one of the most challenging security environments in the world, particularly in Mogadishu. The UN Security Council first imposed an arms embargo on Somalia in 1992, requiring all member states to immediately implement a general and complete arms embargo on all deliveries of weapons and military equipment to Somalia. The UN Monitoring Group on Somalia, established to observe and report

information regarding arms embargo violations and related matters in Somalia, reported in 2007 that "Somalia is literally awash with arms" from various sources, and that the quantity and variety of arms entering the country, in violation of the arms embargo, were greater than at any time since the early 1990s. The security situation in Mogadishu remains volatile. Elsewhere, lawlessness and interclan violence continue in large areas of south-central Somalia.

[6]   The Courts have operated under various names, including the Supreme Council of the Islamic Courts and Union of Islamic Courts.

[7]   Following the African Union's authorization of AMISOM, the UN passed Security Council Resolution 1744, which authorized African Union member states to establish a mission in Somalia for 6 months to carry out the following mandate: (1) to support dialogue and reconciliation in Somalia by assisting with the free movement, safe passage, and protection of relevant individuals; (2) to provide, as appropriate, protection to the Transitional Federal Institutions to help them carry out their functions of government, and security for key infrastructure; (3) to assist, within its capabilities, and in coordination with other parties, with implementation of the National Security and Stabilization Plan, in particular the effective re-establishment and training of all-inclusive Somali security forces; (4) to contribute, as may be requested and within capabilities, to the creation of the necessary security conditions for the provision of humanitarian assistance; and (5) to protect its personnel, facilities, installations, equipment, and mission, and to ensure the security and freedom of movement of its personnel.

[8]   UN officials note that AMISOM's ability to facilitate the provision of humanitarian aid is problematic, as AMISOM troops have been targeted by insurgents in Somalia, and AMISOM lacks the resources to provide this assistance when requested.

[9]   Section 1207 of the National Defense Authorization Act for Fiscal Year 2006 (Pub. L. 109-163) authorizes the Secretary of Defense to provide services and transfer defense articles and funds to the Secretary of State with an aggregate value of up to $100 million per year to facilitate the Secretary of State's provision of reconstruction, security, or stabilization assistance to a foreign country.

[10] The $1 billion in humanitarian assistance represents $745 million in funding for projects included in the UN's consolidated annual appeals for Somalia from 2001 through 2007, as well as an additional $275 million in humanitarian assistance to Somalia from 2001 through 2007

that does not fund projects listed in the appeals. Officials from the UN's Office for the Coordination of Humanitarian Affairs (OCHA) told us that they do not have a complete source of data on donor contributions for humanitarian aid to Somalia that are not included in the UN's appeals. These officials said that while Western donor contributions are largely captured, OCHA does not capture all humanitarian aid provided by the Gulf States, as well as additional bilateral or other funds provided by other donors. Therefore, the figure of over $1 billion is a minimum funding level.

[11] The UN issues an annual appeal through its Consolidated Appeals Process (CAP) for donor funding to support humanitarian needs. The CAP identifies funding requirements in the following humanitarian sectors: agriculture, coordination and support services, economic recovery and infrastructure, education, food, health, mine action, multisector, protection, security, shelter and nonfood items, and water and sanitation. We only report the food aid total provided through the CAP because it is not clear how much of the $275 million reported outside the CAP funded food aid.

[12] The 2008 Consolidated Appeals Process (CAP) for Somalia emphasizes the need for integrated multisectoral programs. Noting that the chronic nutrition crisis in south-central Somalia is the result of the cumulative effect of many factors—including high rates of illness, limited health services, poor water and sanitation services, poor care practices, and reduced availability of and access to nutritious food—the 2008 CAP states that a coordinated response involving all sectors is required.

[13] UN officials also noted that the security situation also usually dictates food assistance as the most appropriate short-term emergency mitigation measure. Furthermore, insecurity—such as that in south-central Somalia—prevents or limits the implementation of agriculture and livelihood initiatives.

[14] The $317 million in U.S. humanitarian assistance to Somalia included in the more than $1 billion in humanitarian assistance from the international community reported for Somalia.

[15] Between fiscal years 2001 and 2007, State's Bureau of Population, Refugees, and Migration also provided almost $119 million in support to Somali refugees in the Horn of Africa and Yemen. In addition, this office provides general funding to respond to refugee crises in Africa, a portion of which assists Somalia.

[16] According to the Food and Agriculture Organization, the Food Security Analysis Unit provides evidence-based analysis of food security, nutrition, and livelihoods in Somalia.

[17] "Global acute malnutrition" is the term used to include all malnourished children whether they have moderate wasting, severe wasting or edema, or some combination of these conditions. Elevated rates of global acute malnutrition directly contribute to increased rates of morbidity and mortality in children under 5 years of age.

[18] The $771 million is reported by the Nairobi-based Somali Support Secretariat, formerly known as the Somalia Aid Coordination Body. The secretariat serves as the main coordinating entity linking UN agencies, NGOs, and donors with relevant Somali ministries. The secretariat reports on annual donor pledges for development assistance. The data in the report are self-reported by donors with verification by the secretariat to ensure accuracy of the reported information. However, secretariat officials reported that the data exclude likely funding from Islamic charities and Gulf States, as they do not report their contributions to the secretariat. Therefore, the total amount of pledged assistance to Somalia during this period is likely higher.

[19] The RDP's framework is aimed at bolstering peace; establishing good governance; improving security and basic social services, such as education and health; and reducing poverty.

[20] In 2007, the U.S. Secretary of State waived legislative restrictions on foreign assistance applicable to the government of Somalia as a result of the country's default on certain loans from the United States. The legislative provisions outlining the restrictions contain authority to waive the restrictions if there is a determination that the assistance to the country is in the U.S. national interest.

[21] We previously developed and used these criteria in other contexts, such as assessments of the Administration's strategies for combating terrorism, rebuilding Iraq, and protecting intellectual property rights. See GAO, *Combating Terrorism: Evaluation of Selected Characteristics in National Strategies Related to Terrorism*, GAO-04-408T (Washington, D.C.: Feb. 3, 2004); *Rebuilding Iraq: More Comprehensive National Strategy Needed to Help Achieve U.S. Goals*, GAO-06-788 (Washington, D.C.: July 11, 2006); and *Intellectual Property: Strategy for Targeting Organized Piracy (STOP) Requires Changes for Long-term Success*, GAO-07-74 (Washington, D.C.: Nov. 8, 2006). Appendix II provides further detail on these characteristics.

[22] We focused our analysis on the Comprehensive Strategy because it was the only one identified as a comprehensive, governmentwide strategy for Somalia.

[23] State's report on the status of implementation of the Comprehensive Strategy through June 2007 does provide general information on DOD's activities related to Somalia, including planning support for AMISOM, public affairs support for the National Reconciliation Congress, and support for counterterrorism capacity-building efforts in the region. Although many of these activities were ongoing when the Comprehensive Strategy was initially issued, they were not included in the strategy.

[24] Our classified report contains further information on the interagency planning process for Somalia.

[25] The International Contact Group on Somalia was established to support the peace and reconciliation efforts in Somalia. Its members include Italy, Kenya, Norway, Sweden, Tanzania, the United Kingdom, and the United States, together with the African Union, European Union, Intergovernmental Authority on Development, League of Arab States, and United Nations.

APPENDIX I

[1] We combined the total funding provided in response to the UN CAP for Somalia from 2001 through 2007 with total humanitarian assistance provided to projects not listed in the appeal to get a minimum of total humanitarian assistance to Somalia for our reporting purposes.

[2] In 2006, the SACB became known as the Coordination of International Support for Somalia, which is supported by the Somali Support Secretariat.

APPENDIX II

[1] GAO, *Combating Terrorism: Evaluation of Selected Characteristics in National Strategies Related to Terrorism*, GAO-04-408T (Washington, D.C.: Feb. 3, 2004).

INDEX

A

access, viii, 5, 9, 13, 23, 28, 29, 30, 33, 41, 59, 61
accountability, 35, 39, 51, 54, 55
accuracy, 49, 62
administration, 12, 21
Africa, ix, 1, 2, 6, 17, 36, 39, 43, 45, 61
African Union, viii, ix, 2, 3, 5, 15, 40, 41, 45, 46, 60, 63
African Union Mission in Somalia (AMISOM), ix, 15, 16, 17, 22, 41, 60, 63
age, 62
agriculture, 25, 27, 61
aid, viii, 2, 5, 10, 16, 20, 23, 24, 25, 27, 30, 31, 32, 46, 47, 54, 60, 61
airports, 32
al Qaeda, 2, 12
appendix, 6
arrest, 30
assessment, 6, 16, 17, 32, 37, 38, 53, 54, 57
assets, 53
assumptions, 38
attacks, 12, 20, 21, 30, 31

attention, 26
auditing, 3, 49
authority, 13, 28, 62
availability, 30, 32, 59, 61

B

basic needs, 41
basic services, 10, 21, 33
benefits, 54
bilateral, vii, 36, 61
birth(s), 9

C

capacity, 5, 15, 17, 18, 20, 21, 23, 25, 27, 28, 31, 32, 33, 41, 63
capacity building, 15, 17, 27
capital, 54
charities, 62
children, 28, 62
Children's Fund, 46
civil service, 21
civil society, 19, 33, 46
closure, 31
collaboration, 55

Combined Joint Task Force-Horn of Africa, ix, 17
commodities, 25, 27
community, viii, 2, 3, 5, 12, 13, 15, 17, 18, 20, 21, 23, 24, 28, 30, 31, 32, 40, 46, 47, 61
components, ix, 3, 6, 35, 48
Comprehensive Regional Strategy, vi, ix, 2, 38, 39, 48, 57, 58
conception, 52
confidence, 13
conflict, viii, 5, 6, 9, 10, 17, 18, 19, 25, 33, 36
congress, 18
Congress, iv, ix, 6, 15, 36, 38, 43, 55, 59, 63
Consolidated Appeals Process (CAP), ix, 24, 46, 47, 61, 63
constraints, 29, 53
construction, 21
contingency, 16
contracts, 2
control, 12, 28
coordination, 3, 21, 26, 27, 28, 32, 39, 52, 55, 60, 61
Copyright, iv
costs, 35, 37, 39, 40, 42, 52
counterterrorism, 18, 36, 63
coverage, 52, 53
credibility, 21, 33

D

data collection, 32
decision makers, 37
decisions, 35
defense, 41, 60
Defense Authorization Act, 35, 60
definition, 38, 53
delivery, 10, 22, 28, 30, 31, 32
demobilization, 17
Department of Defense (DOD), viii, ix, 2, 3, 6, 12, 17, 18, 36, 39, 45, 46, 48, 63

Department of State, 2, 39
desire, 25
detention, 30
development assistance, vii, viii, 2, 5, 23, 32, 33, 45, 47, 62
dictatorship, 10
dietary, ix, 6
dietary intake, ix, 6
Director of National Intelligence, 12
disaster, 27, 36
displaced persons, 25, 41
distribution, 32
donors, 20, 21, 24, 25, 27, 28, 32, 41, 46, 47, 48, 61, 62
draft, 6
droughts, 2, 10
duties, 21

E

economic, 17, 54, 61
economy, 27
edema, 62
education, 26, 33, 61, 62
elders, 19
electronic, iv
electrostatic, iv
embargo, 59
emergency response, 25
engagement, 22, 32, 36, 41, 59
environment, 6, 10, 17, 30, 31, 38, 53
equipment, 16, 54, 59, 60
Eritrea, 19
Ethiopia, vii, 2, 17, 18, 22, 45, 46
European, 32, 46, 63
European Commission, 46
European Union, 32, 63
evacuation, 29
evidence, 3, 47, 49, 62
expertise, 31
experts, 3, 16, 21, 45, 47

F

fees, 31
financial support, 12
Financial Tracking Service (FTS), ix, 46, 47
financing, 18
flexibility, 54
flooding, 31
focusing, 25
food, viii, 2, 5, 9, 23, 24, 25, 26, 27, 30, 32, 41, 46, 47, 59, 61, 62
foreign assistance, 62
freedom, 60
funding, viii, 5, 15, 16, 18, 21, 24, 25, 27, 37, 41, 46, 47, 60, 61, 62, 63
funds, 16, 24, 31, 32, 33, 60, 61

G

gauge, 52, 53
goals, 3, 37, 39, 40, 52, 54, 55
governance, vii, 2, 21, 33, 41, 62
government, vii, viii, ix, 1, 2, 3, 5, 6, 9, 10, 11, 12, 13, 15, 16, 20, 21, 23, 25, 26, 30, 31, 32, 35, 36, 39, 40, 41, 43, 45, 46, 48, 49, 51, 52, 55, 60, 62
Government accountablity Office (GAO), v, vi, vii, viii, 1, 11, 24, 26, 27, 29, 38, 48, 51, 52, 57, 58, 62, 63
grassroots, 33
groups, viii, 1, 5, 10, 18, 19, 20, 28, 41, 53, 59
guidance, 28, 36, 37, 39, 47, 51, 54, 55, 59

H

harassment, 30
health, ix, 6, 25, 26, 28, 30, 33, 41, 61, 62
health care, ix, 6, 26, 30, 41
health services, 28, 61

homes, 9
horizontal integration, 55
House, 1
housing, 41
human, 9, 25, 30, 54
human capital, 54
human development, 9
Human Development Report, 9
human resources, 25
humanitarian, vii, viii, 2, 5, 9, 10, 16, 22, 23, 24, 25, 26, 28, 29, 30, 31, 32, 36, 39, 41, 45, 46, 47, 60, 61, 63
humanitarian aid, 5, 10, 16, 30, 31, 32, 46, 60, 61
humanitarian crises, 10
hygiene, 25

I

implementation, 18, 32, 36, 37, 38, 39, 48, 51, 60, 61, 63
incidence, 28
inclusion, 48
income, 9
independence, 10, 18
indicators, 9, 37, 54
information sharing, 28
information technology, 54
infrastructure, 31, 60, 61
insecurity, ix, 6, 9, 12, 17, 23, 25, 28, 30, 41, 59, 61
inspections, 32
instability, 2, 10
institutions, viii, 5, 10, 21, 23, 32
integration, 3, 26, 37, 40, 51, 55
intellectual property, 62
intellectual property rights, 62
intelligence, 36
internally displaced person(s) (IDP), ix, 25, 27, 28, 30, 41
international, vii, viii, 2, 5, 10, 12, 13, 15, 16, 17, 18, 20, 21, 23, 24, 26, 28, 30, 31, 32, 40, 41, 45, 46, 47, 55, 61
international law, 31

intervention, 12
interviews, 46, 48
Iraq, 62
Islamic, 12, 19, 60, 62
Italy, 32, 46, 63

J

John Warner National Defense
    Authorization Act, 59
Joint Chiefs, 45

K

Kenya, vii, 2, 3, 9, 12, 13, 17, 18, 26, 28,
    31, 32, 37, 45, 46, 48, 63
kidnapping, 30

L

law, ix, 3, 6, 10, 31, 35, 36, 48
lead, 12
leadership, 20
legal, iv
legislation, 2
life expectancy, 9
limitation, 22
literature, 51
loans, 62
local authorities, 31
logistics, 25, 27
long period, 10
long-term, 10, 25
low-income, 9

M

magnetic, iv
malnutrition, viii, 5, 23, 27, 62
management, ix, 3, 6, 36, 37, 39, 52, 54
mandates, 53
market, 27

measures, 3, 6, 39, 52, 53
mechanical, iv
media, 33
messages, 18
Middle East, 48
militant, 12
military, vii, 12, 18, 20, 21, 36, 59
militias, 12, 31
minority, 59
minority groups, 59
missions, 16, 17, 45
morbidity, 62
mortality, 9, 62
mortality rate, 9
movement, 12, 60
multilateral, 36

N

nation, 10
National Defense Authorization Act, 35,
    59, 60
National Reconciliation Congress
    (NRC), ix, 15, 18, 19, 20, 63
National Security Council (NSC), ix, 2,
    3, 7, 48, 55
National Security Strategy, 40
natural, 9
New York, iii, iv, 3, 45
nongovernmental organization(s)
    (NGO), ix, 3, 13, 25, 26, 28, 30, 31,
    33, 46, 62
Norway, 32, 63
nutrition, 25, 61, 62

O

Office for the Coordination of
    Humanitarian Affairs (OCHA), ix, 24,
    29, 46, 47, 61
Office of Management and Budget, 51,
    55
opposition, viii, 1, 5, 10, 18, 19, 20, 41

opposition parties, 20
organization, ix, 12
organizations, vii, 3, 13, 38, 40, 41, 46, 53, 55
oversight, 18, 28, 38, 39, 55

P

Parliament, 13, 19, 21
peacekeeping, viii, 2, 5, 10, 15, 16, 17, 41
peacekeeping forces, 10
performance, 3, 6, 37, 39, 49, 51, 52, 53, 55
performance indicator, 37
periodic, 18
piracy, 31
planning, vii, ix, 2, 3, 6, 16, 35, 36, 37, 39, 41, 45, 46, 48, 51, 63
police, 17, 21
policy makers, 39, 51
political, viii, ix, 2, 5, 6, 9, 12, 15, 16, 17, 18, 19, 20, 21, 22, 23, 32, 36, 39, 40, 41
political stability, 2, 39
poor, 31, 61
population, 9, 21
poverty, 9, 62
power, 10, 12, 59
power sharing, 59
preparedness, 54
president, 10
pressure, 32
priorities, 37, 39, 51, 52, 53
private sector, 46
program, 28, 30, 36
promote, ix, 2, 6, 17, 18, 36, 39, 40
property, viii, 5, 19, 62
property rights, 62
public, 18, 37, 63
public affairs, 18, 63

R

radio, 18
range, viii, ix, 6, 25, 35, 43
recognition, 10
reconcile, 48
reconciliation, viii, 2, 5, 9, 10, 11, 15, 16, 17, 18, 19, 20, 22, 32, 33, 41, 60, 63
reconstruction, 18, 60
Reconstruction and Development Program (RDP), ix, 32, 40, 49, 62
recovery, 17, 61
Red Cross, 25
refugees, 26, 46, 61
regional, ix, 2, 12, 22, 36, 59
relationship(s), 40, 55
reliability, 46
resolution, 16, 31
resource allocation, 37, 39, 51
resource availability, 32
resources, ix, 3, 6, 25, 37, 39, 40, 52, 54, 60
responsibility, iv
risk, ix, 3, 6, 37, 38, 39, 52, 53, 54
risk assessment, 38, 53, 54
risk management, ix, 3, 6, 37, 39, 52, 54
routing, 12
rule of law, 36

S

safety, 30
sanitation, ix, 6, 25, 26, 28, 30, 61
search, 20
secretariat, 48, 62
Secretary of Defense, viii, 6, 43, 45, 60
Secretary of State, viii, 6, 21, 22, 43, 60, 62
Secretary-General, 16, 20
security, viii, 2, 5, 10, 13, 15, 16, 17, 20, 21, 23, 27, 29, 30, 32, 36, 59, 60, 61, 62

Security Council, ix, 2, 16, 31, 48, 55, 59, 60
Senate, 1
series, 10
services, iv
settlements, 27
severity, 16
shape, 20, 37, 51
sharing, 28, 59
shelter, 26, 27, 61
shipping, 31
shortage, viii, 5, 15, 16
sites, 13
social services, 21, 33, 62
society, 19, 33, 46, 54
Somalia, i, iii, v, vi, vii, viii, ix, x, 1, 2, 3, 5, 6, 9, 10, 11, 12, 13, 15, 16, 17, 18, 19, 20, 21, 23, 24, 25, 26, 27, 28, 29, 30, 31, 32, 33, 35, 36, 38, 39, 40, 41, 43, 45, 46, 47, 48, 57, 58, 59, 60, 61, 62, 63
Somalia Aid Coordination Body (SACB), ix, 47, 62, 63
stability, ix, 2, 6, 10, 17, 23, 25, 32, 36, 39, 41
stabilization, 2, 17, 55, 60
stabilize, vii, viii, 2, 5, 15, 45
stakeholders, 13, 20, 22, 37, 51
standards, 3, 49, 51, 54, 55
State Department, 21, 45
strategic, vii, ix, 2, 3, 6, 17, 35, 36, 37, 40, 41, 45, 46, 48, 51, 55
strategic planning, vii, ix, 2, 3, 6, 35, 36, 37, 41, 45, 46, 48, 51
strategies, 32, 35, 37, 40, 51, 52, 54, 55, 62
stress, 53
strikes, 12
Sudan, 16
support services, 61
support staff, 21
survival, 30
Sweden, 32, 63
systems, 10, 27

T

Tanzania, 2, 12, 63
targets, 37
taxation, 31
technical assistance, 18, 21
technology, 54
telephone, 21
territory, 10
terrorism, 62
terrorist, 2, 13, 39
terrorist organization, 13
third party, 12
threat(s), 2, 3, 12, 36, 39, 52, 53, 59
threshold, viii, 6, 23, 27
time, 28, 30, 54, 60
time frame, 54
traffic, 31
training, 18, 36, 60
transition, 20
Transitional Federal Government (TFG), viii, ix, 2, 5, 12, 13, 20, 21, 30, 31, 32, 33, 59
transport, 31
transportation, 27
trucks, 31
trust, 10

U

U.S. Agency for International Development, 2, 45
Uganda, 16
United Kingdom, 46, 63
United Nations(UN), vii, viii, ix, 2, 3, 6, 7, 9, 10, 11, 12, 13, 16, 18, 19, 20, 21, 24, 25, 26, 27, 28, 29, 30, 31, 32, 39, 40, 46, 47, 48, 49, 59, 60, 61, 62, 63
United Nations Department of Peacekeeping Operations (UNDPKO), x, 17
United Nations Development Program (UNDP), x, 17, 18, 21, 33

United Nations High Commissioner for
   Refugees (UNHCR), x, 26, 46
United Nations Political Office for
   Somalia (UNPOS), x, 20
United States, vii, viii, x, 1, 2, 3, 5, 9, 10,
   13, 16, 18, 20, 21, 24, 25, 32, 33, 36,
   40, 42, 48, 62, 63
United States Agency for International
   Development (USAID), x, 2, 3, 6, 7,
   17, 18, 25, 27, 30, 36, 40, 45, 46, 48,
   49, 58

V

vertical integration, 55
vessels, 31
violence, 10, 17, 22, 60
visible, 25

W

War on Terror, 53
warlords, 10, 12
Washington, 3, 45, 62, 63
water, ix, 6, 9, 25, 26, 28, 30, 33, 41, 61
weapons, 59
withdrawal, 10, 19
women, 18
workers, 30
working groups, 28, 53
World Bank, 3, 7, 9, 32, 40, 46, 49
World Food Program, 25
World Food Program (WFP), x, 25, 30
World Health Organization, 46

Y

Yemen, 61